Physical Characteristics of the Bloodhound

(from The Kennel Club breed standard)

Tail: (Stern) Long, thick, tapering to a point, set high with moderate amount of hair underneath. Carried scimitar-fashion, but not curled over the back or corkscrew any time.

Body: Ribs well sprung, chest well let down between forelegs, forming a deep keel. Back and loins strong, the latter deep and slightly arched.

Hindquarters: Thighs and second thighs very muscular. Hocks well let down, bent and squarely set.

Size: Height of adult dogs: 66 cms (26 ins); bitches: 61 cms (24 ins). Dogs usually vary from 63-69 cms (25–27 ins); bitches from 58–63 cms (23–25 ins).

Coat: Smooth, short and weatherproof.

Feet: Strong and well knuckled up.

Bloodhound

◇

By Nona Kilgore Bauer

CONTENTS

PHOTOGRAPHS BY CAROL ANN JOHNSON AND MICHAEL TRAFFORD

with additional photos by Norvia Behling, TJ Calhoun, Carolina Biological Supply,
Doskocil, Isabelle Francais, James Hayden-Yoav, James R Hayden, RBP, Bill Jonas,
Dwight R Kuhn, Dr Dennis Kunkel, Mikki Pet Products, Phototake, Jean Claude Revy,
Dr Andrew Spielman and Alice van Kempen.
Illustrations by Reneé Low.

The publisher wishes to thank Dawn Bather, Joyce Denwood, Gary Freeman,
Iain & Patricia Eason, the Gaillards, the Kretzners, Claudette R Lyons, Celeste Meade,
Michael Moore, Jerrilyn D Petty, Lisa Slinsky, Andrea & Dennis Teirney and the rest of the
owners of the dogs featured in this book.

PUBLISHED IN THE UNITED KINGDOM BY:

INTERPET
P U B L I S H I N G
Vincent Lane, Dorking, Surrey RH4 3YX England

ISBN 1-84286-014-3

This hunting pack of modern-day Bloodhounds from Great Britain speaks volumes about the history of this fascinating breed of scenthound.

History of the
BLOODHOUND

Few breeds of dog can claim the rich and colourful history that distinguishes the scenthounds from other members of the canine clan. In fact, of the many breeds of dog existing in this modern world, the hound is the most ancient. Dating back to the pre-Christian era over 4000 years ago, hound development intertwines with that of man into a most important human-canine evolution.

The very name *hound*—or *Bloodhound*—conjures up impressive, vivid images: a massive animal with its nose to the ground, relentlessly tracking man or beast; a large and threatening dog in determined pursuit of some unseen quarry, whether victim or villain; a ferocious canine beast frothing to attack its prey.

The Bloodhound indeed may be its own combination of these romantic images. The name Bloodhound does not mean 'bloodthirsty beast,' as some believe the term implies. The name is derived from the term 'blooded hound,' which means a dog of pure breeding, whose genes or 'blood' is untainted by other breeds of dog.

The Bloodhound as a specific breed was originally developed and bred centuries ago at the famed St. Hubert Monastery in the mountainous Ardennes region of France. The Bloodhound strain was then perpetuated by church clerics and those members of the nobility who fancied hunting and prized the hounds for their unique abilities.

Thanks to the monastic bent for keeping records through the ages, we have documentation of the hounds that are direct ancestors of the dog we know today as the Bloodhound. In fact, recorded history dating back to 4000 BC offers evidence of massive hound-type canines that were used as war dogs as well as hunting dogs.

The Greek historian, Herodotus, born in the 5th century BC, in his account of the Graeco-Persian wars, wrote of the dog's great value during both times of peace and war. Stone artwork from that era also substantiates historical data showing Bloodhound-type dogs with long tails curled over the back. Herodotus reported that the dogs were especially prized by the monarchs of Mesopotamia (known today as Iraq) and other regions of western Asia.

Another stone carving, dating back even further, to the 7th century BC, and found in the royal palace at Nineveh, the ancient capital of Assyria, depicts powerful hunting dogs who possessed the heavy heads and pendulous ears typical of the Bloodhound.

These dogs' importance to their culture extended far beyond the battle-field. Their scenting prowess and trailing abilities were essential to the food chain, since hunting for food provisions was as vital to survival as was victory in war. So it is understandable that such dogs were highly prized by royalty as well as commoners.

The migration of the hounds

From 1932, this photo shows Bloodhounds that were actual police dogs owned and used by the Chief Constable of Sussex (England).

into Western Europe in later centuries continues to be a matter of speculation. Historians theorise that warriors and migrants took their dogs with them as they migrated into France and England. The Romans described finding magnificent hounds with superb scenting ability when they arrived in Britain in 55 BC. These hounds pursued their quarry with a perseverance unmatched by any they had seen.

Those same hounds were introduced to the French monastery by the crusaders returning from the east, crusaders who also brought other new kinds of animals, new ideas and philosophies. Named the St. Hubertus Branchen, after the monks at that monastery, these hounds were powerful, heavily built dogs, of medium height, who

GENUS *CANIS*
Dogs and wolves are members of the genus *Canis*. Wolves are known scientifically as *Canis lupus* while dogs are known as *Canis domesticus*. Dogs and wolves are known to interbreed. The term *canine* derives from the Latin derived word *Canis*. The term 'dog' has no scientific basis but has been used for thousands of years. The origin of the word 'dog' has never been authoritatively ascertained.

BRAIN AND BRAWN
Since dogs have been inbred for centuries, their physical and mental characteristics are constantly being changed to suit man's desires for hunting, retrieving, scenting, guarding and warming their masters' laps. During the past 150 years, dogs have been judged according to physical characteristics as well as functional abilities. Few breeds can boast a genuine balance between physique, working ability and temperament.

were somewhat long in body. They possessed excellent noses coupled with extraordinary hunting ability. Most were all black with red or fawn markings over their eyes and on their legs, and occasional white marks on the chest. The hounds had superior cold-trailing ability and are the progenitors of all scenthounds known in history or existing now.

A few centuries later, when the Normans from Gaul (France) conquered England in 1066 AD, they brought many of their dogs with them. The St. Hubert's hound was among the conquerors' dogs. There also existed at that

From a 1934 issue
of *Sport and
General*, two
Bloodhounds,
named Eldwick
Meuver and
Malvo, in pursuit
tracing a scent.

From a 1934 issue of *Sport and General*, two Bloodhounds, named Eldwick Meuver and Malvo, in pursuit tracing a scent.

time a few white hounds, called Talbot Hounds (or Southern Hounds), a large dog that was also known for its courage and endurance. Talbots were another strain of hound that allegedly accompanied William the Conqueror to English soil in 1066. William and later his son, Rufus, maintained an extensive breeding programme, breeding hounds that were used primarily for hunting deer, the favoured sport of wealthy noblemen. Some canine historians believe that Talbots were the result of cross-breedings between the St. Hubert's hounds and other white hounds from France.

Never as popular as the black Branchen hound, the white Talbots were kept separate from the blacks, although it is known that in England some St. Hubert's specimens were crossbred with the Talbot. Talbots continued in that country throughout the 18th century before slowly dying out as a result of public rebellion against

ST. HUBERT

St. Hubert is a small town in Belgium in the Province of Luxembourg in the heart of the Ardennes mountain range. The Abbey church contains the shrine of St. Hubert. The church and monastery were founded in the 7th century by Plectrude, wife of Pippin of Herstal. The spot where St. Hubert is alleged to have encountered the stag with the crucifix between its antlers is about 5 miles from the town.

Charles IX, who had bestowed favoured status on that breed.

The St. Hubert Hound was held in such high regard in Europe that the English and French royalty and clerics often filled their kennels with large numbers of the black and tans, often giving them as gifts to high-ranking nobility. One record states that the Earl of Essex maintained a kennel of 800 of these hounds.

The hounds' impressive size and superb scenting ability pressed the breed into service in areas other than hunting for large game such as deer, elk and bear. Many were used as guard dogs to protect private and public property from criminals and violent crime. By the 16th century, Bloodhounds were used extensively to hunt man, particularly sheep thieves and poachers who stalked the Scottish borders. Their man-trailing ability was so valuable that the courts proffered

FRANÇOIS HUBERT

The St. Hubert Branchen hounds were named after the monk François Hubert, who was later elevated to bishop and canonised after his death. Born to the nobility, François was an ardent hunter who maintained a large group of hunting hounds. After François' death, his breeding programme was continued by the abbots who succeeded him.

legal status on the Bloodhound, allowing it to follow a trail anywhere, even directly into a private residence. Their testimony was so highly regarded that if a man refused a Bloodhound entrance to his home, he was assumed to be guilty or associated with the crime.

As happened with all breeds of dogs, civilisation and cultural changes affected society's need and uses for the Bloodhound,

A classic photograph by Fox depicting the high spirit and enthusiasm of the Bloodhound breed for the chase.

The scenthound breeds of Switzerland are close relations to the Bloodhound breed. This is the Bernese Hound, a tricoloured hound known at home as the Berner Laufhund. The term 'laufhund' means 'walking dog.'

sending its popularity into a steep decline. The traditional large estates owned by the upper class were broken up into smaller parcels of land and the surrounding forested areas became smaller, which caused a decrease in the deer and other large-game population. Accordingly, hunters and wealthy sportsmen shifted their interests from hunting deer to hunting smaller and more available game

Here is the Lucernese Hound, known in Switzerland as the Luzerner Laufhund. This breed bears a likeness to the American breed known as the Bluetick Coonhound, and is probably a progenitor of that hunting dog.

law enforcement and a few others were kept in packs by gamekeepers. But the Bloodhound, along with several other breeds of dogs, seemed almost destined for extinction. However, the introduction of the dog show in 1859 proved to be salvation of these beleaguered

The Swiss Hound is known in its native land as the Schweizer Laufhund. Like all the Swiss scenthounds, there is a long and short-legged variety; the short-legged varieties are termed 'nieder-laufhund.'

like the fox, producing a need for smaller, faster hound dogs. Bloodhounds were crossed with a variety of breeds, creating the Foxhound, Harrier, Beagle and other similar breeds that credit their keen noses to their Bloodhound ancestors.

Breed population continued to decline through the mid-19th century. A few remaining Bloodhounds were still used in

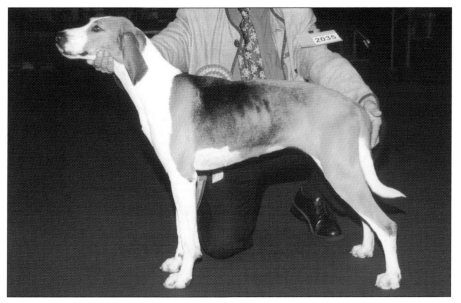

The long-lost Talbot hounds are believed to be descendants of the French scenthounds, such as this modern-day French Tricolour Hound, known in France as the Chien Français Tricolore.

members of the canine community.

That first dog show was held in Newcastle, England, offering an entry of 60 dogs, Pointers and Setters only. The next show, held later that year in Birmingham, was also only for the sporting breeds. Finally, in 1860, the first all-breed show was held, also in Birmingham, and Bloodhounds were among the entries. The rise in the popularity of the dog show gave a logical boost to the popularity of many breeds, and the Bloodhound was no exception.

A secondary positive result was an improvement in breed temperament. Until that time, many specimens lacked an agreeable disposition, with some being either overly aggressive or excessively shy and nervous. Dog shows and the writing of formal breed standards impacted the

THE SWISS ST. HUBERT HOUND

Bearing the same name as the ancient St. Hubert's hound, the St. Hubert Jura Laufhund is counted among the nine scenthound breeds of Switzerland, known as *laufhunden* (dogs that walk beside the hunter). The St. Hubert Jura Laufhund, although a fraction of the size of the Bloodhound, standing 46 to 58 cms (18 to 23 inches) and weighing up to 20 kgs (44 pounds), does share the black/tan coloration as well as key physical features (heavy ears, loose skin and a large head).

Circa 1933, Mrs Russell Cook with Nereholm Falstaff, believed to be the largest Bloodhound in England. This dog would compete with today's dogs, were he still around to do so!

breeders' goals and resulted in more companionable animals who were better suited for the show ring.

During that first decade of dog shows, Bloodhound success on the bench was dominated by lines raised by two noteworthy gentlemen breeders, the Baron Rothschild and Lord Haversham. The first Bloodhound bench champion of record, Druid, owned by Mr T A Jennings, was from those fabled bloodlines. After achieving championship status, Druid, together with the Bloodhound called Welcome, was sold by Mr Jennings to Prince Napoleon as breeding stock for the royal kennels.

All other prize-winning Bloodhounds during the late 1860s were also products of the Rothschild-Haversham breeding programmes. These included the famous Bloodhound Regent, who was owned by Mr Holford, and two other hounds, who were both coincidentally named Rufus. One of these was owned by Mr Edwin Brough, who authored, along with Dr Sidney Turner, the first breed standard for the Bloodhound. Mr Brough later wrote extensively on colour in the Bloodhound, stating that although the most favoured colour seemed to be the black and tan, his personal preference was for the tawny mixed with black markings on the back.

In 1898 the Association of Bloodhound Breeders began to promote man-hunting trials as a sport. By this time, the only breed specimens available for competition were those who had been bred for dog shows and as companion animals. Yet those early trials showed that breeding

THE BISHOP BRANCIE

The name Branchen has been traced back to Bishop Brancie, a prelate who lived in the 7th century. Brancie was a renowned hunter who used such dogs on his hunting forays. One might further speculate that the Branchen may have arrived at the French monastery at the direction of Bishop Brancie, although there is no documentation to that effect.

for purposes other than hunting had not compromised the Bloodhound's scenting ability, as their noses proved to be as keen as ever.

At a man-hunting trial, the hounds were required to run a simple line about a mile long, running the course in pursuit of a scent that had aged for about 15 minutes. Man-trailing proved to be extremely popular with the Bloodhound set, and the sport remains popular even today, with the ultimate prize currently the Brough Cup, a trophy named after Mr Edwin Brough, the author of the first standard. Today's trail is much more difficult and is considered a prestigious event for Bloodhound aficionados.

During the same year that man-trailing was re-introduced, Bloodhounds worked in another, more unusual, capacity, serving as ambulance dogs for the Russian Army Red Cross in the Russo-Japanese War. Decades later, during World War I, they again worked with ambulance teams in Belgium.

Lt Col Richardson with two of his man-tracking Bloodhounds, circa 1930. Note that these working dogs are considerably slighter than our dogs todays.

World War II was another major turning point in the progress and development of not only Bloodhounds but also all breeds of pure-bred dog that suffered serious setbacks during the years from 1939 to 1945. By 1944 the breed had reached a low point of only six registrations and faced near-extinction. Some breeders went to the Foxhound (who was created, after all, from Bloodhound crosses) to restore their lines. Only three English kennels, Brighton, Abingerwood and Barsheen, kept their stock free of such outcross breedings. The white markings that appear occasionally in today's Bloodhound may be a throwback to the Foxhound as well as to the white Talbot Hound that prevailed until the mid-18th century.

HUNTER'S SAINT

St. Hubert is the patron saint of huntsmen. St. Hubert's Day is still celebrated in France, Belgium and Ireland on November 3. The feast day includes a special blessing of the hounds.

Like many of the scenthound breeds of today, the Foxhound owes its keen olfactory senses to its Bloodhound ancestors.

THE BLOODHOUND IN THE UNITED STATES

The Bloodhound first made its mark on the American dog world in 1888 at the prestigious Westminster Kennel Club benched show held in New York City. Three Bloodhounds were exhibited, imported to the States by Mr Brough. Mr J L Winchell of Fairhaven, Vermont, viewed the dogs at the show and was most impressed with their regal stature and noble bearing. He proposed a partnership with Mr Brough and arranged for the import of a breeding pair named Belhus and Rosemary, who became the foundation of the first Bloodhound kennel in America.

Several other prominent breeders took notice of Mr Winchell's move and imported Bloodhounds to add to their kennels and breeding stock. The breed was slow to grow, however, and by 1910 there were only about 200 breed members in the United States. At that time a hound imported from England cost upwards of $2000—an enormous sum in those days—with some fanciers paying up to $5000 for a status symbol Bloodhound. Over the years as the breed became more common, the price dropped to around $100 to $300, a more modest sum for a pure-bred dog.

THE GIFT OF HOUNDS

It has been written that every year for 700 years, the St. Hubert monastery sent three pairs of the black St. Hubert hounds to the reigning king of France. The king, in turn, sent his own gifts of hounds to the first Queen Elizabeth.

BLOODHOUND

ARE YOU READY FOR A BLOODHOUND?

Although the Bloodhound is a most remarkable animal, it is certainly not for everyone, especially the faint of heart. This is a very large dog that requires equally large amounts of space and food. The smaller of the sexes, females grow to be 36–45.5 kgs (80–100 pounds) and stand 61–63 cms (24–25 inches) at the shoulder. The male is consider-ably larger and at full maturity can weigh 45–67 kgs (100–135 pounds) and measure 63–74 cms (25–29 inches) at the shoulder.

Even the Bloodhound pup is not your typical puppy for very long. With a birth weight of 1–2 pounds, the pups grow rapidly, from 4–7 pounds a week, which is as much as many breeds grow in several weeks, and up to one-half to one inch in height per week. So while the Bloodhound puppy is a most irresistible creature, ungainly and incredibly appealing, he is not a 'puppy' (in the normal sense of the word) for very long. He is best raised in a house with a large fenced area; flats in the city are simply not suitable for a dog of such major proportions.

Bloodhounds have very expressive but solemn faces, characterised by heavy wrinkles and very pronounced flews and dewlaps (lips and throat). The eyes are not prominent; in fact,

If raised with children, Bloodhounds grow up to be dependable and trustworthy with children. Oftentimes, though, the dogs don't know their size and weight and can be too exuberant for small children.

The Bloodhound has a very emotive face with heavy wrinkling that gives the breed a noble, profound expression.

charm, as well as to his uniqueness. He can sling saliva across the room with one shake of his enormous head, which is something Bloodhounds do adeptly and frequently. Many owners, in fact, find it convenient to keep 'slobber' towels in strategic locations throughout the house. Moreover, this tendency to lavish slobbery wet kisses on his human friends may not be what everyone might call an attribute!

Yet, despite their slobbery habits, the Bloodhound is a very clean animal. He is fairly easy to house-train if the owner uses patience and intelligence during the toilet-training process. He requires little in the way of bathing, and a monthly tubbing will keep most Bloodhounds clean enough to live with. Like most other breeds of dog, the Bloodhound sheds his coat twice a year.

The Bloodhound's temperament is, or should be, friendly, affectionate and protective. The agreeable factor, however, is somewhat compromised by his enormous size. The amiable Bloodhound who upends himself on both hind legs to lay his paws upon your shoulders to say 'hello' can easily bowl over a child or a small or unprepared adult. Although he is generally very good with children if he is raised with them, his very size, exuberance, and pushy nature

they may appear almost recessed or sunken, and the excessive wrinkling pulls at the lower eyelids, producing a sad and poignant look. Most are black and tan (the tan is sometimes called 'liver'), tawny, or red and tan. The coat is thin, short and hard, typical of the hounds with St. Hubert ancestry. Their long ears hang low and are quite soft to the touch. The long pendulous ears are essential to the Bloodhound's work, acting as scent gatherers while dragging on the ground during a trailing exercise.

Those famous and most generous flews add yet another dimension to the Bloodhound's make him an inappropriate companion for very young children. Despite his great love and devotion for the young members of his human family, he could unintentionally injure a small child during play or rowdy activity. Bloodhounds usually get on well with other dogs; thriving in fact, if they are raised in an environment with other animals. Because they tend to be stubborn, or what some may define as 'determined,' and are inclined to pout when corrected, obedience training can be a challenge.

Of course, this same determination is an asset in the breed's best-known work of man-trailing. Bloodhounds are very aggressive when in pursuit or working on a trail, never giving up until they reach their quarry at the end of the trail.

In contrast to the many common misconceptions about the breed, a well-bred Bloodhound should not be aggressive toward people or other dogs. The ferocious bloodthirsty dogs that were portrayed in the famous American novel, *Uncle Tom's Cabin* by Harriet Beecher Stowe, and in the subsequent movie of the same name, were actually mongrel-type cross-bred hounds with vicious temperaments that are not typical of the usually easygoing Bloodhound. To dispel yet another myth, those same mongrel hounds were the kind of dog used

Happy and easygoing, like most other hounds, Bloodhounds are expressive and affectionate with their masters.

in the early 1900s to track runaway slaves on Southern plantations in the States, a task never performed by a pure-bred Bloodhound. Those events, coupled with other printed accounts and urban legends, unfortunately perpetuated the myth of the Bloodhound as a dangerous and savage beast of pursuit. That simply is not true of this gentle giant breed.

THE MAN-TRAILING BLOODHOUND

Without a doubt, the most common and popular image of the Bloodhound is that of the huge hound sniffing his way through woods and fields to find lost children, escaped convicts or suspected criminals. While the ability to pick up and follow scent is highly instinctive, his unique physical characteristics also contribute to that special talent. His wide nostrils aid in picking up scent; his long, swinging ears scoop the scent up into his nostrils; the generous wrinkles crowning his head help to contain the scent. The loose skin also

BLOODHOUND IN BELGIUM

In Belgium the Bloodhound is still known as the Chien de St Hubert, named after the breed's ancient ancestors.

TAKING CARE

Science is showing that as people take care of their pets, the pets are taking care of their owners. A study in 1998, published in the *American Journal of Cardiology,* found that having a pet can prolong his owner's life. Pet owners generally have lower blood pressure, and pets help their owners to relax and keep more physically fit. It was also found that pets help to keep the elderly connected to their communities.

helps to prevent injury to his head when he is trailing over difficult or rugged terrain. Furthermore, the drooling saliva, which is such an annoyance in the house, creates a steam when combined with heavy breathing on the trail that enhances and raises the scent from the ground.

Beyond that, learning to trail a specific scent on command is a team effort that requires the training and education of both the dog and the handler. Beginning trailing should start in puppyhood, with games like hide-and-seek used as brief training sessions so the pup will not become bored or tired. The pup should be introduced early on to the harness and lead so he learns to associate the trailing work with the sight of the training harness. It is extremely important that any training programme be consistent if the dog is to become proficient in this skill. The more carefully you prepare the dog and the better you learn to read the dog's reaction on a trail, the more successful you will be as a trailing team. There are any number of good books on teaching trailing for search and rescue, as well as organisations that offer camaraderie and advice on tracking trials and other breed activities.

The Bloodhound's man-trailing expertise is recognised in countless stories about man-trailing exploits that put hundreds of criminals behind bars. So celebrated were their successes that many hounds of yore were shot by the criminals they had trailed.

The most famous of man-trailing Bloodhounds, Nick Carter,

Although trailing a scent comes naturally to the Bloodhound, scent training must be introduced early on and be consistently instilled for success.

who was owned, trained and handled by Captain Volney G Mullikin of Lexington, Kentucky, has been credited with over 650 finds that resulted in criminal convictions. At one time Nick Carter held the time record for successfully completing a trail that was over 100 hours old. In 1903 the Lexington *Herald* reported that in a single one-year period, Nick Carter had a 78-percent conviction rate with a record of 126 convictions.

Another pair of famous American Bloodhounds in the early 1900s were two hounds named X-Ray and Jo-Jo, both owned by Dr J B Fulton of Nebraska. In 1902 *Century Magazine* reported that Fulton actually owned 13 trailing Bloodhounds who worked for law enforcement in a five-state area. However, X-Ray and Jo-Jo were his best and held the all-time record for following the longest trail, 135 miles across the state of Kansas, leading the police to the criminal for whom they were hunting.

Not all famous man-trailing exploits pursued the criminal element. Many Bloodhound owners who raised and trained

Though not known for their speed, Bloodhounds can be surprisingly animated and move with speed and alacrity. They are not designed to run for long periods of time, though they can chase down a potential foe when needed.

SENSE OF SMELL

The Bloodhound's sense of smell is so acute that it is said to be 2 million times greater than that of human beings.

man-trailers were frequently called upon to locate missing children. Modern law enforcement in Britain, the United States and other countries still make use of the famous Bloodhound nose despite all of the modern technology involved in the pursuit of criminals. Professionalism in the training and handling of Bloodhounds has given rise to Bloodhound associations in many countries, on many continents, that are affiliated with local police

DO YOU WANT TO LIVE LONGER?

If you like to volunteer, it is wonderful if you can take your dog to a nursing home once a week for several hours. The elder community loves to have a dog with which to visit, and often your dog will bring a bit of companionship to someone who is lonely or somewhat detached from the world. You will be not only bringing happiness to someone else but also keeping your dog busy—and we haven't even mentioned the fact that it has been discovered that volunteering helps to increase your own longevity!

agencies. With their primary goal of training Bloodhounds by time-tested and proven methods, many associations hold seminars to assist in the training and handling of the hounds, as well as offer technical advice from acknowledged experts in the field of man-trailing.

HEREDITARY DISEASE AND HEALTH CONCERNS

Every breed of pure-bred dog faces the challenge of hereditary diseases that threaten its health. Responsible breeders are knowledgeable about the conditions that can be passed on genetically from the dam and sire to the litter, and therefore screen breeding stock before planning a mating. The following hereditary concerns are provided to make the potential owner aware of the problems that face Bloodhounds in the 21st century. Discuss all of them with your chosen breeder and feel confident that your puppy will not be facing difficulties due to irresponsible breeding, failure to screen stock or lack of knowledge.

HIP DYSPLASIA (HD)

Like most working breeds of dog, Bloodhounds are prone to hip dysplasia, which is a potentially crippling disease that affects the hip joints. It is caused by poor bone formation of the femur (upper leg bone) where it fits into

DO YOU KNOW ABOUT HIP DYSPLASIA?

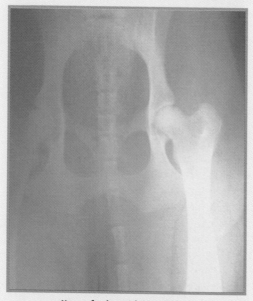

X-ray of a dog with 'Good' hips.

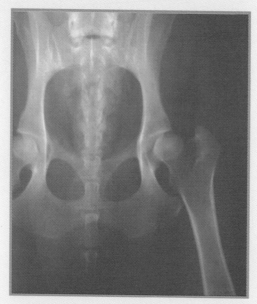

X-ray of a dog with 'Moderate' dysplastic hips.

Hip dysplasia is a fairly common condition found in pure-bred dogs. When a dog has hip dysplasia, its hind leg has an incorrectly formed hip joint. By constant use of the hip joint, it becomes more and more loose, wears abnormally and may become arthritic.

Hip dysplasia can only be confirmed with an x-ray, but certain symptoms may indicate a problem. Your dog may have a hip dysplasia problem if it walks in a peculiar manner, hops instead of smoothly runs, uses its hind legs in unison (to keep the pressure off the weak joint), has trouble getting up from a prone position or always sits with both legs together on one side of its body.

As the dog matures, it may adapt well to life with a bad hip, but in a few years the arthritis develops and many dogs with hip dysplasia become cripples.

Hip dysplasia is considered an inherited disease and only can be diagnosed definitively when the dog is two years old. Some experts claim that a special diet might help your puppy outgrow the bad hip, but the usual treatments are surgical. The removal of the pectineus muscle, the removal of the round part of the femur, reconstructing the pelvis and replacing the hip with an artificial one are all surgical interventions that are expensive, but they are usually very successful. Follow the advice of your veterinary surgeon.

the socket of the hip. Hip dysplasia can be very painful and usually causes arthritis in later years. The condition is thought to be inherited through a complex combination of genetic and environmental factors, and a wise puppy buyer should look for good hips in several generations of a pedigree before purchasing a puppy.

Hip dysplasia is diagnosed by x-ray, with cleared hips receiving a clearance certificate from the British Veterinary Association and The Kennel Club. In the United States, the clearing house for hips is the Orthopedic Foundation for Animals (OFA). All responsible breeders screen their breeding stock for hip dysplasia and obtain the necessary certificates of clearance before breeding any dog.

Current research into the cause(s) and control of hip dysplasia indicates that overfeeding and feeding a diet high in calories (primarily fat) during a large-breed puppy's

SCHWEISSHUNDEN

The black hounds of Ardennes were known as 'schweisshunden'...slow, deliberate, heavy-skinned tracking dogs who trailed with great persistence and possessed exquisite noses and melodious voices. They originally cold-trailed game such as wolf, big cats, deer or trailed wounded game.

DOGS, DOGS, GOOD FOR YOUR HEART!

People usually purchase dogs for companionship, but studies show that dogs can help to improve their owners' health and level of activity, as well as lower a human's risk of coronary heart disease. Without even realising it, when a person puts time into exercising, grooming and feeding a dog, he also puts more time into his own personal health care. Dog owners establish more routine schedules for their dogs to follow, which can have positive effects on a human's health. Dogs also teach us patience, offer unconditional love and provide the joy of having a furry friend to pet!

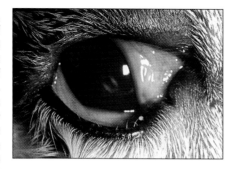

Lower entropion, or rolling in of the eyelid, is causing irritation in the left eye of a young dog. Several extra eyelashes, or distichiasis, are present on the upper lid. Photo courtesy of Prof. Dr Robert L Pfeifer, Jr.

rapid-growth stages may contribute to the onset of HD. Heavy-bodied and overweight puppies are more at risk than pups with very lean conformation. Puppy-raisers are advised to feed a growth food appropriate to those indicators and to keep their puppies trim and lean while still maintaining a proper environment for healthy growth.

ENTROPION

Given their heavily wrinkled brows, it comes as no surprise that Bloodhounds can be prone to entropion, a condition where the eyelid rolls inward, causing the eyelashes to rub the cornea, which is quite painful to the dog. Eventual scarring may cause some

CORRECTIVE SURGERY

Surgery is often used to correct genetic bone diseases in dogs. Usually the problems present themselves early in the dog's life and must be treated before bone growth stops.

---

vision loss. It can be corrected surgically, but affected dogs may pass that gene along to their offspring and should not be bred.

SKIN PROBLEMS

Eczema and dermatitis are skin problems that occur in many breeds, and they can often be tricky problems to solve. Frequently bathing the dog will remove skin oils and will cause the problem to worsen. Allergies to food or to something in the environment can also cause the problem. Consider trying homeopathic remedies in addition to seeing your veterinary surgeon for direction.

GASTRIC DILATATION VOLVULUS (GDV)/BLOAT

Gastric dilatation volvulus, also known as gastric torsion, and more commonly as bloat, is a condition that primarily affects deep-chested breeds of dog. For reasons still unknown to veterinary science, the stomach of the animal suddenly fills with gas and begins to twist, cutting off the blood supply and causing shock and death within a matter of hours. Immediate veterinary care is imperative if the dog is to survive. Because of their physical structure, Bloodhounds are very prone to bloat. The risk can be minimised by feeding several small meals instead of one or two

HOW TO PREVENT BLOAT

Research has confirmed that the structure of deep-chested breeds contributes to their predisposition to bloat. There are several precautions that you can take to reduce the risk of this condition:

- Feed your dog twice daily rather than offer one big meal.
- Do not exercise your dog for at least one hour before and two hours after he has eaten.
- Make certain that your dog is calm and not overly excited while he is eating. It has been proven that nervous or overly excited dogs are more prone to develop bloat.
- Add a small portion of moist meat product to his dried food ration.
- Serve his meals in an elevated bowl stand, which avoids the dog's craning his neck while eating.
- To prevent your dog from gobbling his food too quickly, and thereby swallowing air, put some large (unswallowable) toys into his bowl so that he will have to eat around them to get his food.

For deep-chested dogs that are prone to bloat, an elevated bowl stand is recommended to keep the Bloodhound from craning his neck while eating.

very large meals, and limiting exercise before and after eating, with 'minimise' being the key word in prevention. Every Bloodhound owner should familiarise himself with the physical symptoms of bloat and proper emergency care in the sad event that the dog falls victim to this life-threatening condition.

ALLERGIES

Allergies are common in the Bloodhound, showing up as sensitivities to environmental factors such as pollens, various mites, and/or food products. A good general reference on the different types of allergies and how to treat them is recommended for all Bloodhound owners.

At a dog show, the Bloodhound that the judge deems closest to the breed standard is the winner. It is understood that no dog can ever possess every specific point that the standard defines.

Breed Standard for the
BLOODHOUND

Every breed that is recognised by one of the national or international breed registries is guided by a 'standard,' a detailed description of the dog's physical appearance, its temperament and its natural ability. Breed standards are obviously extremely important to the future of any breed, as without specific guidelines, breeders could alter or completely lose or eliminate the very nature of a breed within just a few generations. Although breeders recognise that it is impossible to produce a perfect dog of any breed, responsible individuals can only do their best to select and breed the best representatives of their chosen breed. Most good breeders also have a general knowledge of genetics and understand the role that dominant and recessive genes play when they plan a litter of pups.

Judges, like breeders, use the standard to make important decisions. It is the breed standard that forms the judge's 'mind's eye' when he is evaluating dogs in the show ring. The judge's choice, the winner of a class, is the dog that most closely conforms to the dog depicted in the breed standard. The notion of a conformation show is to select the dog that 'conforms' most closely to the standard.

THE KENNEL CLUB STANDARD FOR THE BLOODHOUND
(author's comments in italics)

General Appearance: Noble and dignified expression, characterised by solemnity, wisdom and power.

Standing for the judge's inspection, this Bloodhound possesses many of the desired features that the standard enumerates, though the judge's opinion will be the one that counts on the day of the show.

Characteristics: Possesses in a most marked degree every point and characteristic of those dogs who hunt together by scent (Sagaces). Very powerful, standing over more ground than is usual

The head should be narrow in proportion to length, and long in proportion to body.

with hounds of other breeds. Skin thin and loose, especially noticeable about head and neck and where it hangs in deep folds.

'Standing over more ground than other hounds' may be a bit confusing to the novice. This passage refers (at the time the standard was drawn up) to the smaller, more fashionable hounds of that time, Foxhounds, Harriers and Beagles, all of whom are shorter coupled dogs.

Temperament: Affectionate, neither quarrelsome with companions nor with other dogs. Somewhat reserved and sensitive.

Bloodhounds of the past have been known to be quite aggressive, a quality that today is severely faulted, even moreso than the dog who is overtly shy.

Head and Skull: Head narrow in proportion to length and long in proportion to body, tapering slightly from temples to muzzle, this when viewed from above and in front having appearance of being flattened at sides and of being nearly equal in width throughout entire length. In profile upper outline of skull is nearly in same plane as that of foreface. Length from end of nose to stop not less than that from stop to back of occipital protuberance. Entire length of head from posterior part of

occipital protuberance to end of muzzle 30 cms (12 ins) or more in dogs and 28 cms (11 ins) or more in bitches. Skull is long and narrow, with occipital peak very pronounced. Brows not prominent, although owing to set of eyes, may appear to give that appearance. Foreface long, deep and of even width throughout, with square outlines when seen in profile. Head furnished with an amount of loose skin, which in nearly every position appears abundant, but more particularly so when head is carried low; skin then falls into loose pendulous ridges and folds, especially over forehead and sides of face. Nostrils large and open. In front, lips fall squarely making a right angle with upper line of foreface; whilst behind they form deep hanging flews and, being continued into pendant folds of loose skin about neck, constitute the dewlap, which is very pronounced.

In some cases, the weight of the extra loose skin can cause the lower eyelid to hang lower yet and turn outward, causing some of the eye problems typical in the breed. The description of the nostrils, skin and dewlaps are of particular importance since they directly affect the Bloodhound's ability to trail.

Eyes: Medium size, dark brown or hazel, neither sunken nor prominent, the lids being oval in shape and meeting the cornea— front window of the eye— perfectly without any irregularity in their contour. Eyes should be free from any interference from the eyelashes.

Ears: Thin and soft to the touch, long, set on low and falling in graceful folds, lower parts curling inwards and backwards.
'Low ear set' means just below the level of the eye.

Mouth: Jaws strong with a perfect, regular and complete scissor bite, i.e. upper teeth closely overlapping lower teeth and set square to the jaws.

Neck: Long.

Forequarters: Shoulders muscular and well sloped. Forelegs straight, large, round in bone with elbows well set in. Pasterns strong.

Body: Ribs well sprung, chest well let down between forelegs, forming a deep keel. Back and loins strong, the latter deep and slightly arched.

Hindquarters: Thighs and second thighs very muscular. Hocks well let down, bent and squarely set.

Feet: Strong and well knuckled up.

Tail: (Stern) Long, thick, tapering to a point, set high with moderate amount of hair underneath. Carried scimitar-fashion, but not curled over the back or corkscrew any time. When moving carried high.

Bitches rarely do as well as dogs in the show ring, though this lovely Bloodhound bitch has much to offer. From her sweet expression to the tip of her long, tapering tail, she is a lovely specimen.

Gait/Movement: Elastic, swinging free.

Coat: Smooth, short and weatherproof.

Colour: Black and tan, liver and tan (red and tan) and red. Darker colours sometimes interspersed with lighter or badger-coloured hair and sometimes flecked with white. Small amounts of white permissible on chest, feet and tip of tail.

Size: Height of adult dogs: 66 cms (26 ins); bitches: 61 cms (24 ins). Dogs usually vary from 63-69 cms (25–27 ins); bitches from 58–63 cms (23–25 ins). Mean average weight of adult dogs in fair condition 41 kgs (90 lbs); bitches: 36 kgs (80 lbs). Dogs attain the weight of 50 kgs (110 lbs); bitches: 45.5 kgs (100 lbs). Hounds of the maximum height and weight preferred, providing that quality, proportion and balance combine.

Faults: Any departure from the foregoing points should be considered a fault and the seriousness with which the fault should be regarded should be in exact proportion to its degree.

Note: Male animals should have two apparently normal testicles fully descended into the scrotum.

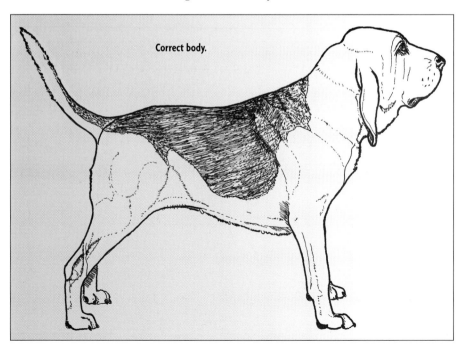

Correct body.

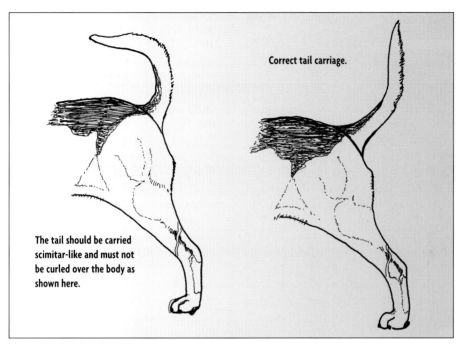

Correct tail carriage.

The tail should be carried scimitar-like and must not be curled over the body as shown here.

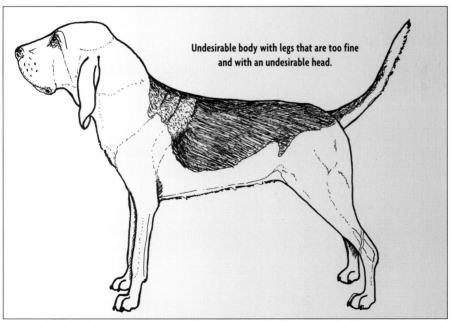

Undesirable body with legs that are too fine and with an undesirable head.

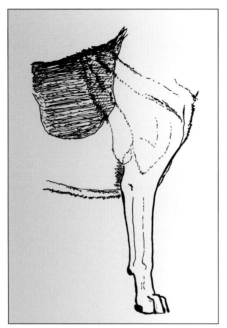

Correct front.

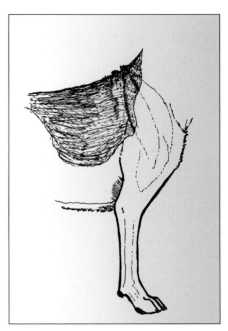

Incorrect front. Shoulder too steep and weak pastern.

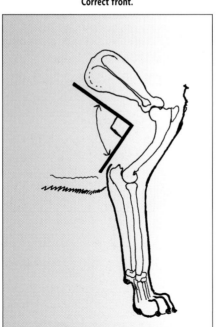

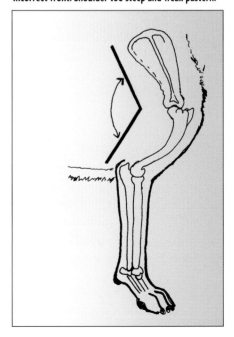

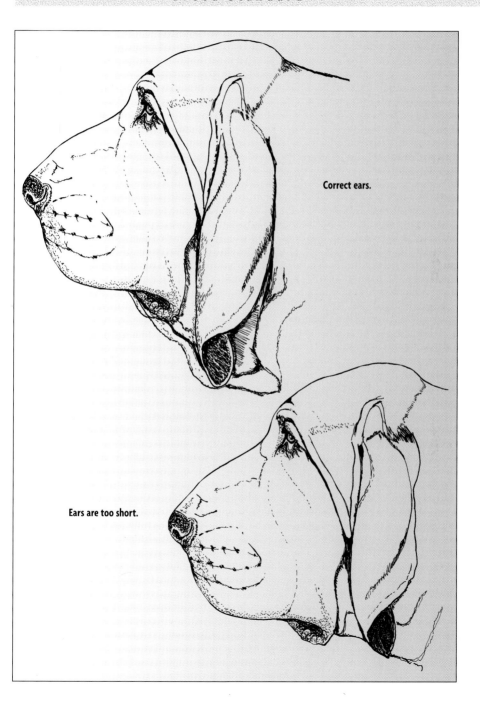

Correct ears.

Ears are too short.

Your Puppy

BLOODHOUND

ADDING A BLOODHOUND TO YOUR FAMILY

Living with a dog, especially a Bloodhound, is a major, life-altering decision, one that should be researched with at least as much diligence as shopping for a new home, car or major appliance. Give yourself this short quiz to see if you are truly prepared to share your life with a Bloodhound.

Why do you desire this particular breed of dog? There are about 330 recognised breeds of pure-bred dog available, about half of which can be readily found in the UK, in the USA and in some countries on the Continent. You have selected this large scenthound because it possesses unique qualities beyond those of all the other breeds you have investigated. A Bloodhound is truly the right animal for you, your family and your living situation. You are committed to providing this Bloodhound puppy with an ideal life.

Do you fully understand the animal, its temperament and its physical and emotional needs? (Yes, dogs definitely have emotional needs.) Have you read as much as possible on the breed to learn the advantages and disadvantages of living with this dog? You can also attend dog

---

PREPARING FOR PUP

Unfortunately, when a puppy is bought by someone who does not take into consideration the time and attention that dog ownership requires, it is the puppy who suffers when he is either abandoned or placed in a shelter by a frustrated owner. So all of the 'homework' you do in preparation for your pup's arrival will benefit you both. The more informed you are, the more you will know what to expect and the better equipped you will be to handle the ups and downs of raising a puppy. Hopefully, everyone in the household is willing to do his part in raising and caring for the pup. The anticipation of owning a dog often brings a lot of promises from excited family members: 'I will walk him every day,' 'I will feed him,' 'I will house-train him,' etc., but these things take time and effort, and promises can easily be forgotten once the novelty of the new pet has worn off.

PUPPY SELECTION

Your selection of a good puppy can be determined by your needs. A show potential or a good pet? It is your choice. Every puppy, however, should be of good temperament. Although show-quality puppies are bred and raised with emphasis on physical conformation, responsible breeders strive for equally good temperament. Do not buy from a breeder who concentrates solely on physical beauty at the expense of personality.

like conformation or obedience in mind. Perhaps you have also considering the possibility of entering the dog in man-trailing events like tracking, search and rescue for law enforcement or search and rescue as a volunteer. Since the Bloodhound is such a talented animal, you must consider giving the dog ample opportunity to 'be all that he can be.'

And finally, if all these answers are in the affirmative, how do you find the right dog or puppy?

shows and trailing events if possible, to better acquaint yourself with members of the breed and talk to the exhibitors and owners about their dogs.

Do you have the time, facilities and funds to support this breed of dog? You will need a house, large garden area, good fencing, time for walks, canine hygiene and exercise, and money for food, veterinary care and emergency medical treatment if necessary. Strong fencing is especially essential since most Bloodhounds are either climbers or diggers and will do either or both in order to follow their noses.

What are your goals for the dog and will you be able to achieve them? You have considered whether your Bloodhound will be just a family pet or if you have some type of competition

LOCATING A BREEDER

Finding a good breeder is the first key to success in living with any breed of dog. The only source for a puppy is a breeder who specialises in Bloodhounds, whether you purchase a puppy directly from the breeder or decide to acquire a dog from a rescue scheme at a breeder's

Let your children participate in the selection of a puppy. This adorable pair of puppies is doing a fine job of beguilng this handsome youngster.

THE BLOODHOUND LITTER

There is considerable variation in the size of a Bloodhound dam's litter. The average litter size can range from a small litter of 4 or 5 pups to as many as 15. A litter of 9 or 10 is common.

kennel. Reputable breeders raise puppies because they know and love their chosen breed, and the puppies' welfare is their top priority. They spend considerable time socialising their puppies to prepare them for life outside the whelping box. They also are very discriminating about the people who buy their pups and require assurance that each new owner will provide an happy, healthy environment for their Bloodhound babies. Thus, when searching for a pup, you should expect a good breeder to ask you as many

questions as you ask of him. If he makes no enquiries about you or your intentions, move forward and continue looking elsewhere until you find a knowledgeable breeder who cares about his puppies more than your money. The Kennel Club, veterinary surgeons in your area, dog shows and breed clubs are all good sources to check when looking for a pup of any breed.

FINDING AND SELECTING A BLOODHOUND PUPPY

Be sure to ask any breeder you interview about the health of his puppies, and if the sire and dam have proper certificates of clearance. Ask to see those papers as well as The Kennel Club registration papers and the puppy's pedigree (essentially the family tree of the dog).

Scrutinise the pup's environment for cleanliness, stimuli and human contact. A dark corner in

There is considerable variation in the size of a Bloodhound dam's litter. The dam's task in raising up to 15 puppies is exhausting, and she will likely need some human aid.

the basement is not an appropriate place to raise a litter of pups. Make sure the pups have received their first distemper shot. Puppies should remain with their dam until they are at least seven weeks of age; good breeders seldom send puppies home before that time. Some breeders of show puppies may want to hold their pups a little longer in order to better evaluate those pups with show potential.

Look for heavy bones, big, tight feet, clear eyes and nose, long ears that reach to the tip of the nose, a square lip and prominent loose skin around the head and neck. If you are looking for a man-trailing Bloodhound, arrange for the breeder to help you test the pups to find the best nose in the litter. After spending seven weeks raising and observing his Bloodhound brood, the breeder should be able to identify which of the pups first or always puts its head down to sniff and search for its mother or its food dish.

COMMITMENT OF OWNERSHIP

After considering all of these factors, you have most likely already made some very important decisions about selecting your puppy. You have chosen a Bloodhound, which means that you have decided which characteristics you want in a dog and what type of dog will

DOCUMENTATION
Two important documents you will get from the breeder are the pup's pedigree and registration certificate. The breeder should register the litter and each pup with The Kennel Club, and it is necessary for you to have the paperwork if you plan on showing or breeding in the future.

Make sure you know the breeder's intentions on which type of registration he will obtain for the pup. There are limited registrations which may prohibit the dog from being shown, bred or competing in non-conformation trials such as Working or Agility if the breeder feels that the pup is not of sufficient quality to do so. There is also a type of registration that will permit the dog in non-conformation competition only.

On the reverse side of the registration certificate, the new owner can find the transfer section, which must be signed by the breeder.

best fit into your family and lifestyle. If you have selected a breeder, you have gone a step further—you have done your research and found a responsible, conscientious person who breeds quality Bloodhounds and who should become a reliable source of help as you and your puppy adjust to life together. If you have

observed a litter in action, you have obtained a firsthand look at the dynamics of a puppy 'pack' and, thus, you have learned about each pup's individual person-ality—perhaps you have even found one that particularly appeals to you.

However, even if you have not yet found the Bloodhound puppy of your dreams, observing pups will help you learn to recognise certain behaviour and to determine what a pup's behaviour indicates about his temperament. You will be able to pick out which pups are the leaders, which ones are less outgoing, which ones are confident, which ones are shy, playful, friendly, aggressive, etc. Equally as important, you will learn to recognise what an healthy pup should look and act like. All of these things will help you in your search, and when you find

PUPPY APPEARANCE

Your puppy should have a well-fed appearance but not a distended abdomen, which may indicate worms or incorrect feeding, or both. The body should be firm, with a solid feel. The skin of the abdomen should be pale pink and clean, without signs of scratching or rash. Check the hind legs to make certain that dewclaws were removed, if any were present at birth.

Finding the Bloodhound puppy of your dreams will make the search well worth the effort. Discuss your intentions for the puppy with the breeder as you pursue your dream pup.

the Bloodhound that was meant for you, you will know it!

Researching your breed, selecting a responsible breeder and observing as many pups as possible are all important steps on the way to dog ownership. It may seem like a lot of effort...and you have not even taken the pup home yet! Remember, though, you cannot be too careful when it comes to deciding on the type of dog you want and finding out about your prospective pup's background. Buying a puppy is not—or should not be—just another whimsical purchase. This is one instance in which you actually do get to choose your own family! You may be thinking that buying a puppy should be fun—it should not be so serious and so much work. Keep in mind that your puppy is not a cuddly stuffed toy or decorative lawn ornament; rather, he is a living creature who will become a real

INSURANCE

Many good breeders will offer you insurance with your new puppy, which is an excellent idea. The first few weeks of insurance will probably be covered free of charge or with only minimal cost, allowing you to take up the policy when this expires. If you own a pet dog, it is sensible to take out such a policy as veterinary fees can be high, although routine vaccinations and boosters are not covered. Look carefully at the many options open to you before deciding which suits you best.

ARE YOU A FIT OWNER?
If the breeder from whom you are buying a puppy asks you a lot of personal questions, do not be insulted. Such a breeder wants to be sure that you will be a fit provider for his puppy.

member of your family. You will come to realise that, while buying a puppy is a pleasurable and exciting endeavour, it is not something to be taken lightly. Relax...the fun will start when the pup comes home!

Always keep in mind that a puppy is nothing more than a baby in a furry disguise...a baby who is virtually helpless in a human world and who trusts his owner for fulfilment of his basic needs for survival. In addition to food, water and shelter, your pup needs care, protection, guidance and love. If you are not prepared to commit to this, then you are not prepared to own a dog.

Wait a minute, you say. How hard could this be? All of my neighbours own dogs and they seem to be doing just fine. Why should I have to worry about all of this? Well, you should not worry about it; in fact, you will probably find that once your Bloodhound pup gets used to his new home, he will fall into his place in the family quite naturally. However, it never hurts to emphasise the commitment of dog ownership. With some time and patience, it is really not too difficult to raise a curious and exuberant Bloodhound pup to become a well-adjusted and well-mannered adult dog—a dog that could be your most loyal friend.

PREPARING PUPPY'S PLACE IN YOUR HOME
Researching your breed and finding a breeder are only two aspects of the 'homework' you will have to do before taking your Bloodhound puppy home. You will also have to prepare your home and family for the new addition. Much as you would prepare a nursery for a newborn baby, you will need to designate a place in your home that will be the puppy's own. How you prepare your home will depend on how much freedom the dog will be allowed. Whatever you decide, you must ensure that he has a place that he can 'call his own.'

When you bring your new puppy into your home, you are bringing him into what will become his home as well. Obviously, you did not buy a puppy with the intentions of catering to his every whim and allowing him to 'rule the roost,' but in order for a puppy to grow into a stable, well-adjusted dog, he has to feel comfortable in his surroundings. Remember, he is leaving the warmth and security of his mother and littermates, as well as the familiarity of the only place he has ever known, so it is important to make his transition as easy as possible.

By preparing a place in your home for the puppy, you are making him feel as welcome as possible in a strange new place. It should not take him long to get used to it, but the sudden shock of being transplanted is somewhat traumatic for a young pup. Imagine how a small child would feel in the same situation—that is how your puppy must be feeling. It is up to you to reassure him and to let him know, 'Little chap, you are going to like it here!'

WHAT YOU SHOULD BUY

CRATE

To someone unfamiliar with the use of crates in dog training, it may seem like punishment to shut a dog in a crate, but this is not the case at all. Although all breeders do not advocate crate training, more and more breeders and trainers are recommending crates as preferred tools for show puppies as well as pet puppies.

Crates are not cruel—crates have many humane and highly effective uses in dog care and training. For example, crate training is a popular and successful house-training method.

DID YOU KNOW?

Bloodhound breeders rarely release puppies until they are seven to eight weeks of age. Toy breeds, however, are not released until around 12 weeks, given their petite sizes. If a breeder has a puppy that is 12 weeks of age or older, it is likely well socialised and house-trained. Be sure that it is otherwise healthy before deciding to take it home.

PHOTO COURTESY OF DOSKOCIL

providing him with something a little more luxurious than what his early ancestors enjoyed.

As far as purchasing a crate, the type that you buy is up to you. It will most likely be one of the two most popular types: wire or fibreglass. There are advantages and disadvantages to each type. For example, a wire crate is more open, allowing the air to flow through and affording the dog a view of what is going on around him, while a fibreglass crate is sturdier. Both can double as travel crates, providing protection for the dog.

A Bloodhound needs a very large crate, one that will accommodate a dog of 45.5 kgs (100 pounds) or more. Purchase an extra-large size at approximately 71 cms wide by 122 cms high by 79 cms long (28 inches wide by 48 inches high by 31 inches long). It's best to order the crate before your puppy is due to arrive, in case the pet-supply outlet or pet shop does not stock such a large model.

In addition, a crate can keep your dog safe during travel and, perhaps most importantly, a crate provides your dog with a place of his own in your home. It serves as a 'doggie bedroom' of sorts—your Bloodhound can curl up in his crate when he wants to sleep or when he just needs a break. Many dogs sleep in their crates overnight. With soft bedding and his favourite toy, a crate becomes a cosy pseudo-den for your dog. Like his ancestors, he too will seek out the comfort and retreat of a den—you just happen to be

BEDDING

Veterinary bedding in the dog's crate will help the dog feel more at home, and you may also like to pop in a small blanket. First, this will take the place of the leaves, twigs, etc., that the pup would use in the wild to make a den; the pup can make his own 'burrow' in the crate. Although your pup is

CRATE TRAINING TIPS

During crate training, you should partition off the section of the crate in which the pup stays. If he is given too big an area, this will hinder your training efforts. Crate training is based on the fact that a dog does not like to soil his sleeping quarters, so it is ineffective to keep a pup in a crate that is so big that he can eliminate in one end and get far enough away from it to sleep. Also, you want to make the crate den-like for the pup. Blankets and a favourite toy will make the crate cosy for the small pup; as he grows, you may want to evict some of his 'roommates' to make more room.

It will take some coaxing at first, but be patient. Given some time to get used to it, your pup will adapt to his new home-within-a-home quite nicely.

Toys

Toys are a must for dogs of all ages, especially for curious playful pups. Puppies are the 'children' of the dog world, and what child does not love toys? Chew toys provide enjoyment for both dog and owner—your dog will enjoy playing with his favourite toys, while you will enjoy the fact that they distract him from chewing on your expensive shoes and leather sofa. Puppies love to chew; in fact, chewing is a physical need for pups as they are teething, and everything looks appetising! The full range of your possessions— from old tea towel to Oriental carpet—are fair game in the eyes of a teething pup. Puppies are not all that discerning when it comes to finding something literally to

far removed from his den-making ancestors, the denning instinct is still a part of his genetic makeup. Second, until you take your pup home, he has been sleeping amid the warmth of his mother and littermates, and while a blanket is not the same as a warm, breathing body, it still provides heat and something with which to snuggle. You will want to wash your pup's bedding frequently in case he has a toileting 'accident' in his crate, and replace or remove any blanket that becomes ragged and starts to fall apart.

Don't forget the toys! Don't wait until your puppy finds his own objects to play with. Provide him with safe chew toys that will distract him from eating your possessions.

TOYS, TOYS, TOYS!

With a big variety of dog toys available, and so many that look like they would be a lot of fun for a dog, be careful in your selection. It is amazing what a set of puppy teeth can do to an innocent-looking toy, so, obviously, safety is a major consideration. Be sure to choose the most durable products that you can find. Hard nylon bones and toys are a safe bet, and many of them are offered in different scents and flavours that will be sure to capture your dog's attention. It is always fun to play a game of catch with your dog, and there are balls and flying discs that are specially made to withstand dog teeth.

'sink their teeth into'—everything tastes great!

Bloodhound puppies are fairly active chewers and only the hardest, strongest toys should be offered to them. Breeders advise owners to resist stuffed toys, because they can become de-stuffed in no time. The overly excited pup may ingest the stuffing, which is neither digestible nor nutritious.

Similarly, squeaky toys are quite popular, but must be avoided for the Bloodhound. Perhaps a squeaky toy can be used as an aid in training, but not for free play. If a pup 'disembowels' one of these, the small plastic squeaker inside can be dangerous if swallowed. Monitor the condition of all your pup's toys carefully and get rid of any that have been chewed to the point of becoming potentially dangerous.

Be careful of natural bones, which have a tendency to splinter into sharp, dangerous pieces. Also be careful of rawhide, which can turn into pieces that are easy to swallow and become a mushy mess on your carpet.

LEAD

A nylon lead is probably the best option, as it is the most resistant to puppy teeth should your pup take a liking to chewing on his lead. Of course, this is a habit that should be nipped in the bud, but, if your pup likes to chew on his lead, he has a very slim chance of being able to chew through the strong nylon. Nylon leads are also lightweight, which is good for a young Bloodhound who is just getting used to the idea of walking on a lead.

For everyday walking and safety purposes, the nylon lead is a good choice. As your pup grows up and gets used to walking on the lead, you may want to purchase a flexible lead. These leads allow you to extend the length to give the dog a broader area to explore or to shorten the length to keep the dog near you. Of course, there are leads designed for training purposes and specially made leather harnesses. These are not necessary for routine walks, but should be

Your local pet shop will have an array of leads from which you can select those leads that best suit your needs.

introduced to the Bloodhound puppy who is destined for a career as a man-trailer or tracking dog.

COLLAR

Your pup should get used to wearing a collar all the time since you will want to attach his ID tags to it; plus, you have to attach the lead to something! A lightweight nylon collar is a good choice. Make certain that the collar fits snugly enough so that the pup cannot wriggle out of it, but is loose enough so that it will not be uncomfortably tight around the pup's neck. You should be able to fit a finger between the pup's neck and the collar. It may take some time for your pup to get used to

FINANCIAL RESPONSIBILITY

Grooming tools, collars, leashes, dog beds and, of course, toys will be an expense to you when you first obtain your pup, and the cost will continue throughout your dog's lifetime. If your puppy damages or destroys your possessions (as most puppies surely will!) or something belonging to a neighbour, you can calculate additional expense. There is also flea and pest control, which every dog owner faces more than once. You must be able to handle the financial responsibility of owning a dog.

When purchasing bowls for your Bloodhound, select the largest and most indestructible bowls you can find. Your pet shop should have a wide selection for you to make a good choice.

PHOTO COURTESY OF MIKKI PET PRODUCTS.

wearing the collar, but soon he will not even notice that it is there. Choke collars are made for training, but are not recommended for the Bloodhound, who has too much loose skin around his neck for such a collar to be effective.

FOOD AND WATER BOWLS

Your pup will need two bowls, one for food and one for water. You may want two sets of bowls, one for indoors and one for outdoors, depending on where the dog will be fed and where he will be spending time. Stainless steel or sturdy plastic bowls are popular choices. Plastic bowls are more chewable, but dogs tend not to chew on the steel variety, which also can be sterilised. It is important to buy sturdy bowls since anything is in danger of being chewed by puppy teeth and you do not want your dog to be constantly chewing apart his bowl (for his safety and for your purse!).

For your Bloodhound, investigate bowls that are designed for dogs with large ears (which keep the dog's ears out of his food and water) as well as bowl stands (which elevate the dog's bowls so that he doesn't have to crane his neck to eat; ideal for breeds prone to bloat). Your pet shop should be able to assist you in finding these items that are well worth the extra expense for your Bloodhound.

CHOOSE AN APPROPRIATE COLLAR

The **BUCKLE COLLAR** is the standard collar used for everyday purposes. Be sure that you adjust the buckle on growing puppies. Check it every day. It can become too tight overnight! These collars can be made of leather or nylon. Attach your dog's identification tags to this collar.

The **CHOKE COLLAR** is made for training, but is not appropriate for use on a Bloodhound. It is constructed of highly polished steel so that it slides easily through the stainless steel loop. The idea is that the dog controls the pressure around its neck and he will stop pulling if the collar becomes uncomfortable. It should never be left on a dog when not training.

The **HALTER** is for a trained dog that has to be restrained to prevent running away, chasing a cat and the like. Considered the most humane of all collars, it is frequently used on smaller dogs for which collars are not comfortable.

CHEMICAL TOXINS

Scour your garden and garage for potential doggie dangers. Remove weed killers, pesticides and antifreeze materials. Antifreeze is highly toxic and just a few drops can kill even a large dog. The sweet taste attracts the animal, who will quickly consume it from the floor or curbside.

CLEANING SUPPLIES

Drooling can make a home very untidy! Be ready to wipe up your pup's mouth on a regular basis, not just after eating and drinking. Have towels designated for this purpose. Until a pup is house-trained, you will be doing a lot of cleaning from the other end as well. 'Accidents' will occur, which is acceptable in the beginning stages of toilet training because the puppy does not know any better. All you can do is be prepared to clean up any accidents and messes as soon as they happen. Old rags, towels, newspapers and a safe disinfectant are good to have on hand.

BEYOND THE BASICS

The items previously discussed are the bare necessities. You will find out what else you need as you go along—grooming supplies, flea/tick protection, baby gates to partition a room, etc. These things will vary depending on your situation, but it is important that you have everything you need to feed and make your Bloodhound comfortable in his first few days at home.

PUPPY-PROOFING YOUR HOME

Aside from making sure that your Bloodhound will be comfortable in your home, you also have to make sure that your home is safe for your Bloodhound. This means taking precautions that your pup will not get into anything he should not get into and that there is nothing within his reach that may harm him should he sniff it, chew it, inspect it, etc. This probably seems obvious since, while you are primarily concerned with your pup's safety, at the same time you do not want your belongings to be ruined. Breakables should be placed out of reach if your dog is to have full run of the house. If he is to be limited to certain places within the house, keep any potentially dangerous items in the 'off-limits' areas.

An electrical cord can pose a danger should the puppy decide to taste it—and who is going to convince a pup that it would not make a great chew toy? Cords should be fastened tightly against the wall. If your dog is going to spend time in a crate, make sure that there is nothing near his crate that he can reach if he sticks his curious little nose or paws through the openings. Just as you would with a child, keep all household cleaners and chemicals where the pup cannot reach them. Bloodhounds are not known for voracious chewing, although, like all pups, they will gnaw on your best shoe if you turn your back.

It is also important to make sure that the outside of your home is safe. Of course, your puppy should never be unsupervised, but a pup let loose in the garden will want to run and explore, and he should be granted that freedom. Do not let a fence give you a false sense of security; you would be surprised at how crafty (and persistent) a dog can be in working out how to dig under and squeeze his way through small holes, or to jump or climb over a fence. The remedy is to make the fence well embedded into the ground and high enough so that it really is impossible for your dog to get over it (about 2 metres

should suffice). Be sure to repair or secure any gaps in the fence. Check the fence periodically to ensure that it is in good shape and make repairs as needed; a very determined pup may return to the same spot to 'work on it' until he is able to get through.

TOXIC PLANTS

Many plants can be toxic to dogs. If you see your dog carrying a piece of vegetation in his mouth, approach him in a quiet, disinterested manner, avoid eye contact, pet him and gradually remove the plant from his mouth. Alternatively, offer him a treat and maybe he'll drop the plant on his own accord. Be sure no toxic plants are growing in your own garden.

NATURAL TOXINS

Examine your grass and garden landscaping before bringing your puppy home. Many varieties of plants have leaves, stems or flowers that are toxic if ingested, and you can depend on a curious Bloodhound to investigate them. Ask your vet for information on poisonous plants or research them at your library.

Bloodhounds are not jumpers, climbers or diggers by nature; however, they have often been known to do all three. They will follow their noses relentlessly, and that may lead them over or under the back fence.

FIRST TRIP TO THE VET

You have selected your puppy, and your home and family are ready. Now all you have to do is collect your Bloodhound from the breeder and the fun begins, right? Well...not so fast. Something else you need to plan is your pup's first trip to the veterinary surgeon. Perhaps the breeder can recommend someone in the area who knows Bloodhounds, or maybe you know some other Bloodhound owners who can suggest a good vet. Either way, you should have an appointment arranged for your pup before you pick him up.

The pup's first visit will consist of an overall examination to make sure that the pup does not have any problems that are not apparent to you. The veterinary surgeon will also set up a schedule for the pup's vaccinations; the breeder will inform you of which ones the pup has already received and the vet can continue from there.

INTRODUCTION TO THE FAMILY

Everyone in the house will be excited about the puppy's coming home and will want to pet him and play with him, but it is best to make the introduction low-key so as not to overwhelm the puppy. He is apprehensive already. It is the first time he has been separated from his mother and the breeder, and the ride to your home is likely to be the first time he has been in a car. The last thing you want to do is smother him, as this will only frighten him

HOW VACCINES WORK

If you've just bought a puppy, you surely know the importance of having your pup vaccinated, but do you understand how vaccines work? Vaccines contain the same bacteria or viruses that cause the disease you want to prevent, but they have been chemically modified so that they don't cause any harm. Instead, the vaccine causes your dog to produce antibodies that fight the harmful bacteria. Thus, if your pup is exposed to the disease in the future, the antibodies will destroy the viruses or bacteria.

The Bloodhound's large ears can be a hindrance to the hungry hound. Be sure to clean your dog's ears after he has eaten or drunk.

further. This is not to say that human contact is not extremely necessary at this stage, because this is the time when a connection between the pup and his human family is formed. Gentle petting and soothing words should help console him, as well as just putting him down and letting him explore on his own (under your watchful eye, of course).

The pup may approach the family members or may busy himself with exploring for a while. Gradually, each person should spend some time with the pup, one at a time, crouching down to get as close to the pup's level as possible, letting him sniff their hands and petting him gently. He definitely needs human attention and he needs to be

FEEDING TIPS

You will probably start feeding your pup the same food that he has been getting from the breeder; the breeder should give you a few days' supply to start you off. Although you should not give your pup too many treats, you will want to have puppy treats on hand for coaxing, training, rewards, etc. Be careful, though, as a small pup's calorie requirements are relatively low and a few treats can add up to almost a full day's worth of calories without the required nutrition.

touched—this is how to form an immediate bond. Just remember that the pup is experiencing many things for the first time, at the same time. There are new people, new noises, new smells and new things to investigate, so be gentle, be affectionate and be as comforting as you can be.

PUP'S FIRST NIGHT HOME

You have travelled home with your new charge safely in his crate. He's been to the vet for a thorough check-up; he's been weighed, his papers have been examined and perhaps he's even been vaccinated and wormed as well. He's met (and licked!) the whole family, including the excited children and the less-than-happy cat. He's explored his area, his new bed, the garden and anywhere else he's been permitted. He's eaten his first meal at home and relieved himself in the proper place. He's heard lots of new sounds, smelled new friends and seen more of the outside world than ever before... and that was just the first day! He's worn out and is ready for bed...or so you think!

It's puppy's first night home and you are ready to say 'Good night.' Keep in mind that this is his first night ever to be sleeping alone. His dam and littermates are no longer at paw's length and he's a bit scared, cold and lonely. Be reassuring to your new family member, but this is not the time to spoil him and give in to his inevitable whining.

Puppies whine. They whine to let others know where they are

Socialising your Bloodhound pup means giving him a variety of experiences to make him well rounded in the company of other dogs and people.

PUPPY PROBLEMS

The majority of problems that are commonly seen in young pups will disappear as your dog gets older. However, how you deal with problems when he is young will determine how he reacts to discipline as an adult dog. It is important to establish who is boss (hopefully it will be you!) right away when you are first bonding with your dog. This bond will set the tone for the rest of your life together.

and hopefully to get company out of it. Place your pup in his new bed or crate in his designated area and close the door. Mercifully, he may fall asleep without a peep. When the inevitable occurs, however, ignore the whining—he is fine. Be strong and keep his interest in mind. Do not allow yourself to feel guilty and visit the pup. He will fall asleep eventually.

Many breeders recommend placing a piece of bedding from the pup's former home in his new bed so that he recognises and is comforted by the scent of his littermates. Others still advise placing a hot water bottle in the bed for warmth. The latter may be a good idea provided the pup doesn't attempt to suckle—he'll get good and wet, and may not fall asleep so fast.

Puppy's first night can be somewhat stressful for both the pup and his new family. Remember that you are setting the tone of night-time at your house. Unless you want to play with your pup every night at 10 p.m., midnight and 2 a.m., don't initiate the habit. Your family will thank you, and so will your pup!

PREVENTING PUPPY PROBLEMS

SOCIALISATION

Now that you have done all of the preparatory work and have helped your pup get accustomed to his new home and family, it is about time for you to have some fun! Socialising your Bloodhound pup gives you the opportunity to show off your new friend, and your pup gets to reap the benefits of being an adorable wrinkly creature that people will want to pet and, in general, think is absolutely precious!

Besides getting to know his new family, your puppy should be exposed to other people, animals and situations. This will help him become well adjusted as he grows up and less prone to being timid or fearful of the new things he will encounter. As pack dogs, Bloodhounds are not generally aggressive with other dogs, but they will not back down from an altercation. They should be socialised with other dogs while

PROPER SOCIALISATION

The socialisation period for puppies is from age 8 to 16 weeks. This is the time when puppies need to leave their birth family and take up residence with their new owners, where they will meet many new people, other pets, etc. Failure to be adequately socialised can cause the dog to grow up fearing others and being shy and unfriendly due to a lack of self-confidence.

still in puppyhood to condition them to proper canine social behaviour. Of course, your pup must not come into close contact with dogs you don't know well until his course of injections is fully complete.

Your pup's socialisation began with the breeder, but now it is your responsibility to continue it. The socialisation he receives until the age of 12 weeks is the most critical, as this is the time when he forms his impressions of the outside world. Be especially careful during the eight-to-ten-week-old period, also known as the fear period. The interaction he receives during this time should be gentle and reassuring. Lack of socialisation, and/or negative experiences during the socialisa-tion period, can manifest itself in fear and aggression as the dog grows up. Your puppy needs lots of positive interaction, which of course includes human contact, affection, handling and exposure to other animals.

Once your pup has received his necessary vaccinations, feel free to take him out and about (on his lead, of course). Walk him around the neighbourhood, take him on your daily errands, let people pet him, let him meet other dogs and pets, etc. Puppies do not have to try to make friends; there will be no shortage of people who will want to introduce themselves. Just make sure that you carefully supervise each meeting. If the neighbourhood children want to say hello, for example, that is great—children and pups most often make great companions. However, sometimes an excited child can unintentionally handle a pup too roughly, or an overzealous pup can playfully nip a little too hard.

You want to make socialisation experiences positive ones. What a pup learns during this very formative stage will affect his attitude toward future encounters. You want your dog to be comfortable around everyone. A pup that has a bad experience with a child, for example, may grow up to be a dog that is shy around or aggressive toward children.

CONSISTENCY IN TRAINING

Dogs, being pack animals, naturally need a leader, or else they try to establish dominance in their packs. When you welcome a dog into your family, the choice of who becomes the leader and who becomes the 'pack' is entirely up to you! Your pup's intuitive quest for dominance, coupled with the fact that it is nearly impossible to look at an adorable Bloodhound pup with his 'puppy-dog' face and not cave in, give the pup almost an unfair advantage in getting the upper hand!

A pup will definitely test the waters to see what he can and cannot do. Do not give in to those

MANNERS MATTER

During the socialisation process, a puppy should meet people, experience different environments and definitely be exposed to other canines. Through playing and interacting with other dogs, your puppy will learn lessons, ranging from controlling the pressure of his jaws by biting his littermates to the inner-workings of the canine pack that he will apply to his human relationships for the rest of his life. That is why removing a puppy from its litter too early can be detrimental to the pup's development.

pleading eyes—stand your ground when it comes to disciplining the pup and make sure that all family members do the same. It will only confuse the pup if Mother tells him to get off the sofa when he is

young developing pup than to wait until the pup's bad behaviour becomes the adult dog's bad habit. There are some problems that are especially prevalent in puppies as they develop.

NIPPING

As puppies start to teethe, they feel the need to sink their teeth into anything available...unfortunately, that usually includes your fingers, arms, hair and toes. You may find this behaviour cute for the first five seconds...until you feel just how sharp those puppy teeth are. Nipping is something you want to discourage immediately and consistently with a firm 'No!' (or whatever number of firm 'Nos' it takes for him to understand that you mean business). Then, replace your finger with an appropriate chew toy.

Praise and encourage your Bloodhound puppy when he has done well. Correct him firmly and fairly when he starts to engage in an inappropriate activity, such as nipping or chewing one of your garments.

used to sitting up there with Father to watch the nightly news. Avoid discrepancies by having all members of the household decide on the rules before the pup even comes home...and be consistent in enforcing them! Early training shapes the dog's personality, so you cannot be unclear in what you expect.

COMMON PUPPY PROBLEMS

The best way to prevent puppy problems is to be proactive in stopping an undesirable behaviour as soon as it starts. The old saying 'You can't teach an old dog new tricks' does not necessarily hold true, but it is true that it is much easier to discourage bad behaviour in a

MEET THE WORLD

Thorough socialisation includes not only meeting new people but also being introduced to new experiences such as riding in the car, having his coat brushed, hearing the television, walking in a crowd—the list is endless. The more your pup experiences, and the more positive the experiences are, the less of a shock and the less frightening it will be for your pup to encounter new things.

While this behaviour is merely annoying when the dog is young, it can become dangerous as your Bloodhound's adult teeth grow in and his jaws develop, and he continues to think it is okay to gnaw on human appendages. Your Bloodhound does not mean any harm with a friendly nip, but he also does not know his own strength.

CRYING/WHINING

Your pup will often cry, whine, whimper, howl or make some type of commotion when he is left alone. The Bloodhound is blest with a large, resonant voice, and the puppy soon learns how to use his howl for many occasions. This is basically his way of calling out for attention to make sure that you know he is there and that you have not forgotten about him. Your puppy feels insecure when he is left alone, when you are out of the house and he is in his crate or when you are in another part of the house and he cannot see you. The noise he is making is an expression of the anxiety he feels at being alone, so he needs to be taught that being alone is okay. You are not actually training the dog to stop making noise; rather, you are training him to feel comfortable when he is alone and thus removing the need for him to make the noise.

This is where the crate with cosy bedding and a toy comes in

TRAINING TIP

Training your puppy takes much patience and can be frustrating at times, but you should see results from your efforts. If you have a puppy that seems untrainable and is never able to focus on the lesson, take him to a trainer or behaviourist. The dog may have a personality problem that requires the help of a professional, or perhaps you need help in learning how to train your dog.

Your Bloodhound
puppy depends
on you for
everything... from
his food and
water to his
education and
entertainment.

able in his crate. On that note, it is extremely important that the crate is never used as a form of punishment; this will cause the pup to view the crate as a negative place, rather than as a place of his own for safety and retreat.

Accustom the pup to the crate in short, gradually increasing time intervals in which you put him in the crate, maybe with a treat, and stay in the room with him. If he cries or makes a fuss, do not go to him, but stay in his sight. Gradually he will realise that staying in his crate is all right without your help, and it will not be so traumatic for him when you are not around. You may want to leave the radio on softly when you leave the house; the sound of human voices may be comforting to him.

handy. You want to know that your pup is safe when you are not there to supervise, and you know that he will be safe in his crate rather than roaming freely about the house. In order for the pup to stay in his crate without making a fuss, he first needs to be comfort-

CHEWING TIPS

Chewing goes hand in hand with nipping in the sense that a teething puppy is always looking for a way to soothe his aching gums. In this case, instead of chewing on you, he may have taken a liking to your favourite shoe or something else which he should not be chewing. Again, realise that this is a normal canine behaviour that does not need to be discouraged, only redirected. Your pup just needs to be taught what is acceptable to chew on and what is off limits. Consistently tell him NO when you catch him chewing on something forbidden and give him a chew toy. Conversely, praise him when you catch him chewing on something appropriate. In this way you are discouraging the inappropriate behaviour and reinforcing the desired behaviour. The puppy chewing should stop after his adult teeth have come in, but an adult dog continues to chew for various reasons—perhaps because he is bored, perhaps to relieve tension or perhaps he just likes to chew. That is why it is important to redirect his chewing when he is still young.

DIETARY AND FEEDING CONSIDERATIONS

Today the choices of food for your Bloodhound are many and varied. There are simply dozens of brands of food in all sorts of flavours and textures, ranging from puppy diets to those for seniors. There are even hypoallergenic and low-calorie diets available. Because your Bloodhound's food has a bearing on coat, health and temperament, it is essential that the most suitable diet is selected for a Bloodhound of his age. It is fair to say, however, that even experienced owners can be perplexed by the enormous range of foods available. Only understanding what is best for your dog will help you reach an informed decision.

Dog foods are produced in three basic types: dried, semi-moist and tinned. Dried foods are useful for the cost-conscious, for overall they tend to be less expensive than semi-moist or tinned foods. Dried foods also contain the least fat and the most preservatives. In general, tinned foods are made up of 60–70 percent water, while semi-moist

ones often contain so much sugar that they are perhaps the least preferred by owners, even though their dogs seem to like them.

When selecting your dog's diet, three stages of development must be considered: the puppy stage, the adult stage and the senior or veteran stage.

PUPPY STAGE

Puppies instinctively want to suck milk from their mother's teats; a normal puppy will exhibit this behaviour just a few moments following birth. If puppies do not

Deciding what to feed your growing Bloodhound is tantamount to knowing that your dog will have the nutrients he needs to develop properly in body and mind. Feeding affects the dog's growth, behaviour and coat quality.

FOOD PREFERENCE

Selecting the best dried dog food is difficult. There is no majority consensus among veterinary scientists as to the value of nutrient analyses (protein, fat, fibre, moisture, ash, cholesterol, minerals, etc.). All agree that feeding trials are what matter, but you also have to consider the individual dog. The dog's weight, age and activity level, and what pleases his taste, all must be considered. It is probably best to take the advice of your veterinary surgeon. Every dog's dietary requirements vary, even during the lifetime of a particular dog.

Breeders' opinions vary on whether or not you should supplement your dog's dried food with meat or vegetables. Dogs do appreciate a little variety in their diets, so you may choose to stay with the same brand but vary the flavour. Alternatively, you may wish to add a little flavoured stock to give a difference to the taste.

attempt to suckle within the first half-hour or so, they should be encouraged to do so by placing them on the nipples, having selected ones with plenty of milk. This early milk supply is important in providing the essential colostrum, which protects the puppies during the first eight to ten weeks of their lives. Although a mother's milk is much better than any milk formula, despite there being some excellent ones available, if the puppies do not feed, the breeder will have to feed them by hand. For those with less experience, advice from a veterinary surgeon is important so that not only the right quantity of milk is fed but also that of correct quality, fed at suitably frequent intervals, usually every two hours during the first few days of life.

Puppies should be allowed to nurse from their mothers for about the first six weeks, although, starting around the third or fourth week, the breeder will begin to introduce small portions of suitable solid food. Most breeders like to introduce alternate milk and meat meals initially, building up to weaning time.

Many breeders advocate supplementing the puppy's diet with vitamin powders, cooked eggs, cottage cheese, ground meat, cod liver oil and other supplements. Still others rely on the research and wisdom of commercial food manufacturers to determine the best diet for a growing Bloodhound pup. There is great value in both feeding philosophies. Your veterinary surgeon should be your best guide to proper nutrition for your own pup. Adequate portion size is important. Your puppy will grow at a rate of 4 to 7 pounds a week. Bloodhounds should remain on an appropriate puppy diet until at least one year of age.

ADULT DIETS

It is safe to say, however, that by the time your Bloodhound is a year old, he will be eating upwards of six cups of commercial dog meal, plus whatever additives you have been advised to offer. Again you should rely upon your veterinary surgeon or dietary specialist to recommend an acceptable maintenance diet. Major dog food manufacturers specialise in this type of food, and it is merely necessary for you to select the one best suited to your

GRAIN-BASED DIETS

Some less expensive dog foods are based on grains and other plant proteins. While these products may appear to be attractively priced, many breeders prefer a diet based on animal proteins and believe that they are more conducive to your dog's health. Many grain-based diets rely on soy protein, which may cause flatulence (passing gas).

There are many cases, however, when your dog might require a special diet. These special requirements should only be recommended by your veterinary surgeon.

dog's needs. Active dogs may have different requirements than sedate dogs.

SENIOR DIETS

As dogs get older, their metabolism changes. The older dog usually exercises less, moves

Discuss food choices with your breeder. Rely on his experience with the Bloodhound and don't vary too far from his and your vet's recommendations.

TEST FOR PROPER DIET

A good test for proper diet is the colour, odour and firmness of your dog's stool. A healthy dog usually produces three semi-hard stools per day. The stools should have no unpleasant odour. They should be the same colour from excretion to excretion.

more slowly and sleeps more. This change in lifestyle and physiological performance requires a change in diet. Switch to a senior formula at about six years of age.

Since these changes take place slowly, they might not be recognisable. What is easily recognisable is weight gain. By continuing to feed your dog an adult-maintenance diet when it is slowing down metabolically, your dog will gain weight. Obesity in an older dog compounds the health problems that already accompany old age.

DO DOGS HAVE TASTE BUDS?

Watching a dog 'wolf' or gobble his food, seemingly without chewing, leads an owner to wonder whether their dogs can taste anything. Yes, dogs have taste buds, with sensory perception of sweet, salty and sour. Puppies are born with fully mature taste buds.

TIPPING THE SCALES

Good nutrition is vital to your dog's health, but many people end up over-feeding or giving unnecessary supplements. Here are some common doggie diet don'ts:

• Adding milk, yoghurt and cheese to your dog's diet may seem like a good idea for coat and skin care, but dairy products are very fattening and can cause indigestion.
• Diets high in fat will not cause heart attacks in dogs but will certainly cause your dog to gain weight.
• Most importantly, don't assume your dog will simply stop eating once he doesn't need any more food. Given the chance, he will eat you out of house and home!

As your dog gets older, few of his organs function up to par. The kidneys slow down and the intestines become less efficient. These age-related factors are best handled with a change in diet and a change in feeding schedule to give smaller portions that are more easily digested. There is no single best diet for every older dog. While many dogs do well on light or senior diets, other dogs do better on puppy diets or other special premium diets such as lamb and rice. Be sensitive to your senior Bloodhound's diet, as this will help control other problems that may arise with your old friend.

WATER

Just as your dog needs proper nutrition from his food, water is an essential 'nutrient' as well. Water keeps the dog's body properly hydrated and promotes normal function of the body's systems. During house-training it is necessary to keep an eye on how much water your Bloodhound is drinking, but once he is reliably trained he should have access to clean fresh water at all times, especially if you feed dried food. Make certain that the dog's water bowl is clean, and change the water often.

EXERCISE

Exercising your Bloodhound can be enjoyable and healthy for both of you. Adult Bloodhounds need brisk, long walks once or twice a day to keep them in good physical condition and prevent boredom. Do not subject the growing puppy to vigorous exercise or long walks. Stress on the growing Bloodhound puppy's muscles, bones and ligaments can have adverse effects on proper development, possibly aggravating hip dysplasia or another orthopaedic condition.

The Bloodhound is physically mature by two years of age, continuing to fill out until three years of age. Although the puppy may no longer look like a puppy, his bones are still growing, so be wary of causing harm to his expanding frame. As the dog

DRINK, DRANK, DRUNK—MAKE IT A DOUBLE

In both humans and dogs, as well as most living organisms, water forms the major part of nearly every body tissue. Naturally, we take water for granted, but without it, life as we know it would cease.

For dogs, water is needed to keep their bodies functioning biochemically. Additionally, water is needed to replace the water lost while panting. Unlike humans, who are able to sweat to dissipate heat, dogs must pant to cool down, thereby losing the vital water from their bodies needed to regulate their body temperatures. Humans lose electrolyte-containing products and other body-fluid components through sweating; dogs do not lose anything except water.

Water is essential always, but especially so when the weather is hot or humid or when your dog is exercising or working vigorously.

reaches adulthood, the speed and distance of the walks can be increased as long as they are both kept reasonable and comfortable for both of you.

Play sessions in the garden and letting the dog run free in the garden under your supervision also are sufficient forms of exercise for the Bloodhound. Fetching games can be played indoors or out; these are excellent for giving your dog active play that he will enjoy. Chasing things that move comes naturally to dogs of all breeds. When your Bloodhound runs after the ball or object, praise him for picking it up and encourage him to bring it back to you for another throw. Never go to the object and pick it up yourself, or you'll soon find that you are the one retrieving the objects rather than the dog! If you

LET THE SUN SHINE
Your dog needs daily sunshine for the same reason people do. Pets kept inside homes with curtains drawn against the sun suffer from 'SAD' (Seasonal Affected Disorder) to the same degree as humans. We now know that sunlight must enter the iris and thus progress to the pineal gland to regulate the body's hormonal system. When we live and work in artificial light, both circadian rhythms and hormone balances are disturbed.

choose to play games outdoors, you must have a securely fenced-in garden and/or have the dog attached to at least a 25-foot light line for security. You want your Bloodhound to run, but not run away!

Free running in your fenced garden is an ideal way to give your Bloodhound enjoyable, stress-free exercise.

What are you feeding your dog?

Read the label on your dog food. Many dog foods only advise what 50—55% of the contents are, leaving the other 45% in doubt.

Calcium 1.3%
Fatty Acids 1.6%
Crude Fibre 4.6%
Moisture 11%
Crude Fat 14%
Crude Protein 22%
45.5% ? ? ?

GROOMING

BRUSHING

A natural bristle brush or a hound glove can be used for regular routine brushing. Daily brushing is effective for removing dead hair and stimulating the dog's natural oils to add shine and an healthy look to the coat. Although the Bloodhound's coat is hard and close, it does require a five-minute once-over to keep it looking its shiny best. Regular grooming sessions are also a good way to spend time with your dog. Many dogs grow to like the feel of being brushed and will enjoy the daily routine.

Beyond brushing, Bloodhounds have few grooming needs other than caring for their very large, pendulous ears and deep-set eyes. The ears are low-slung and fold about the side of the head, which can lead to rather heavy wax build-up. Just a wipe or two

An undercoat rake facilitates the removal of dead hair from the Bloodhound's coat during shedding season. Purchase only top-quality durable grooming tools for use on your Bloodhound.

Bear in mind that an overweight dog should never be suddenly over-exercised; instead he should be encouraged to increase exercise slowly. Not only is exercise essential to keep the dog's body fit, it is essential to his mental well-being. A bored dog will find something to do, which often manifests itself in some type of destructive behaviour. In this sense, exercise is essential for the owner's mental well-being as well!

EXERCISE ALERT!
You should be careful where you exercise your dog. Many countryside areas have been sprayed with chemicals that are highly toxic to both dogs and humans. Never allow your dog to eat grass or drink from puddles on either public or private grounds, as the run-off water may contain chemicals from sprays and herbicides.

inside the ear will keep them clean, and this should be performed daily or, at the very least, weekly. Many hounds are subject to more waxy ears than others, so regular and frequent ear checks are a good owner policy.

BATHING

Bloodhounds are generally very clean dogs who need bathing only about once a month. For all dogs, long hair and short, bathing is essential for healthy skin and an healthy, shiny coat. Again, like most anything, if you accustom your pup to being bathed as a puppy, it will be second nature by the time he grows up. You want your dog to be at ease in the bath or else it could end up a wet,

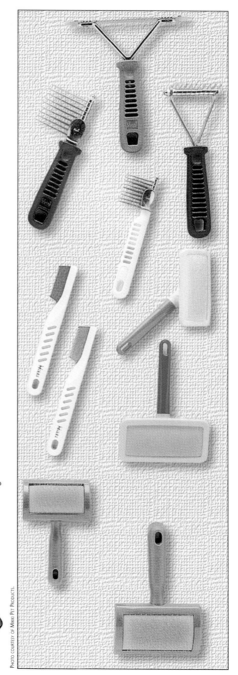

Your local pet shop should have a variety of tools with which you can groom your Bloodhound.

PHOTO COURTESY OF MIKKI PET PRODUCTS.

GROOMING EQUIPMENT

How much grooming equipment you purchase will depend on how much grooming you are going to do. Here are some basics:

• Natural bristle brush
• Hound glove
• Metal comb
• Shedding rake
• Blaster
• Rubber mat
• Dog shampoo
• Spray hose attachment
• Ear cleaner
• Cotton wipes
• Towels
• Nail clippers

Use a bristle brush, preferably on a daily basis, to keep your Bloodhound's coat shiny and healthy.

Use a bristle brush, preferably on a daily basis, to keep your Bloodhound's coat shiny and healthy.

soapy, messy ordeal for both of you!

Brush your Bloodhound thoroughly before wetting his coat. This will get rid of any debris in the coat before you start to bath. Make certain that your

dog has a good non-slip surface on which to stand. Begin by wetting the dog's coat, checking the water temperature to make sure that it is neither too hot nor too cold. A shower or hose attachment is necessary for thoroughly wetting and rinsing the coat.

Next, apply shampoo to the dog's coat and work it into a good lather. Wash the head last, as you do not want shampoo to drip into the dog's eyes while you are washing the rest of his body. You should use only a shampoo that is made for dogs. Do not use a product made for human hair. Work the shampoo all the way down to the skin. You can use this opportunity to check the skin for any bumps, bites or other abnormalities. Do not neglect any area of the body—get all of the hard-to-reach places.

Once the dog has been thoroughly shampooed, he requires an equally thorough rinsing. Shampoo left in the coat can be irritating to the dog's skin. Protect his eyes from the shampoo by shielding them with your hand and directing the flow of water in the opposite direction. You should also avoid getting water in the ear canal. Be prepared for your dog to shake out his coat— you might want to stand back, but make sure you have a hold on the dog to keep him from running through the house.

EAR CLEANING

Since the Bloodhound's ears are so large, they should be cleaned on a regular basis. Use a cotton wipe and ear powder made especially for dogs. Do not probe into the ear canal with a cotton

bud, as this can cause injury. Be on the lookout for any signs of infection or ear-mite infestation. If your Bloodhound has been shaking his head or scratching at his ears frequently, this usually indicates a problem. If the dog's ears have an unusual odour, this is a sure sign of mite infestation or infection, and a signal to have his ears checked by the veterinary surgeon.

NAIL CLIPPING

Your Bloodhound should be accustomed to having his nails trimmed at an early age since nail clipping will be part of your maintenance routine throughout his life. Not only does it look nicer, but long nails can scratch

If you introduce your Bloodhound puppy to the nail clipping routine, you will be blest with an adult that doesn't mind having his monthly pedicure.

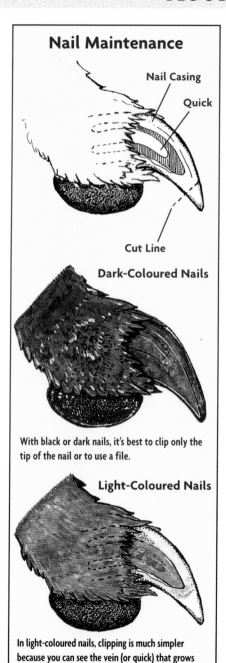

Nail Maintenance

Nail Casing

Quick

Cut Line

Dark-Coloured Nails

With black or dark nails, it's best to clip only the tip of the nail or to use a file.

Light-Coloured Nails

In light-coloured nails, clipping is much simpler because you can see the vein (or quick) that grows inside the casing.

someone unintentionally. Also, a long nail has a better chance of ripping and bleeding, or causing the feet to spread. A good rule of thumb is that if you can hear your dog's nails clicking on the floor when he walks, his nails are too long.

Before you start cutting, make sure you can identify the 'quick' in each nail. The quick is a blood

PEDICURE TIP

A dog that spends a lot of time outside on a hard surface, such as cement or pavement, will have his nails naturally worn down and may not need to have them trimmed as often, except maybe in the colder months when he is not outside as much. Regardless, it is best to get your dog accustomed to the nail-trimming procedure at an early age so that he is used to it. Some dogs are especially sensitive about having their feet touched, but if a dog has experienced it since puppyhood, it should not bother him.

vessel that runs through the centre of each nail and grows rather close to the end. The quick will bleed if accidentally cut, which will be quite painful for the dog as it contains nerve endings. Keep some type of clotting agent on hand, such as a styptic pencil or styptic powder (the type used for shaving). This will stop the bleeding quickly when applied to the end of the cut nail. Do not panic if you cut the quick, just stop the bleeding and talk soothingly to your dog. Once he has calmed down, move on to the next nail. It is better to clip a little at a time, particularly with black-nailed dogs.

Hold your pup steady as you begin trimming his nails; you do not want him to make any sudden movements or run away. Talk to him soothingly and stroke him as you clip. Holding his foot in your hand, simply take off the end of each nail with one swift clip. You should purchase nail clippers that are made for use on dogs; the guillotine-style clippers are recommended for your Bloodhound.

TRAVELLING WITH YOUR DOG

CAR TRAVEL

You should accustom your Bloodhound to riding in a car at an early age. You may or may not take him in the car often, but at the very least he will need to go to

MOTION SICKNESS

*If life is a motorway...*your dog may not want to come along for the ride! Some dogs experience motion sickness in cars that leads to excessive salivation and even vomiting. In most cases, your dog will fare better in the familiar, safe confines of his crate. To desensitise your dog, try going on several short jaunts before trying a long trip. If your dog experiences distress when riding in the vehicle, drive with him only when absolutely necessary, and do not feed him or give him water before you go.

ON THE ROAD

If you are going on a long motor trip with your dog, be sure the hotels are dog-friendly. Many hotels do not accept dogs. Also take along some ice that can be thawed and offered to your dog if he becomes overheated. Most dogs like to lick ice.

the vet, and you do not want these trips to be traumatic for the dog or troublesome for you. The safest way for a dog to ride in the car is in his crate. If he uses a crate in the house, you can use the same crate for travel.

Put the pup in the crate and see how he reacts. If he seems uneasy, you can have a passenger hold him on his lap while you drive. Another option for car travel is a specially made safety harness for dogs, which straps the dog in much like a seat belt. Do not let the dog roam loose in the vehicle—this is very dangerous! If you should stop short, your dog can be thrown and injured. If the dog starts climbing on you and pestering you while you are driving, you will not be able to concentrate on the road. It is an unsafe situation for everyone— human and canine.

For long trips, be prepared to stop to let the dog relieve himself. Take with you whatever you need to clean up after him, including some paper kitchen towels and perhaps some old towelling for use should he have a toileting accident in the car or suffer from travel sickness.

AIR TRAVEL

While it is possible to take a dog on a flight within Britain, this is fairly unusual and advance permission is always required. The dog will be required to travel in a fibreglass crate and you should always check in advance with the airline regarding specific requirements. To help put the dog at ease, give him one of his favourite toys in the crate. Do not feed the dog for at least six hours before the trip in order to minimise his need to relieve himself. However, certain regulations specify that water must always be made available to the dog in the crate.

Make sure your dog is properly identified and that your contact information appears on his ID tags and on his crate. Animals travel in a different area of the plane than human passengers, so every rule must be strictly followed so as to prevent the risk of getting separated from your dog.

HOLIDAYS AND BOARDING

So you want to take a family holiday—and you want to include *all* members of the family. You would probably make arrangements for accommodation ahead of time anyway, but this is especially important when travelling with a dog. You do not want to make an overnight stop at the only place around for miles, only to find out that they do not allow dogs. Also, you do not want to reserve a place for your family without confirming that you are travelling with a dog, because, if it is against their policy, you may end up without a place to stay.

Alternatively, if you are travelling and choose not to bring your Bloodhound, you will have to make arrangements for him while you are away. Some options are to take him to a neighbour's house to stay while you are gone, to have a trusted neighbour pop in often or stay at your house or to bring your dog to a reputable boarding kennel. If you choose to board him at a kennel, you should visit in advance to see the facilities provided and where the dogs are kept. Are the dogs' areas spacious and kept clean? Talk to some of the employees and observe how they treat the dogs—do they spend time with the dogs, play with them, exercise them, etc.? Also find out the kennel's policy on vaccinations and what they require. This is for all of the dogs' safety, since there is a greater risk of diseases being passed from dog to dog when dogs are kept together.

IDENTIFICATION

Your Bloodhound is your valued companion and friend. That is why you always keep a close eye on him and you have made sure that he cannot escape from the garden or wriggle out of his collar and run away from you. However, accidents can happen and there may come a time when your dog unexpectedly becomes separated from you. If this unfortunate event should occur, the first thing on your mind will be finding him. Proper identification, including an ID tag, a tattoo and possibly a microchip, will increase the chances of his being returned to you safely and quickly.

Select a reputable local boarding kennel before you actually need it. Be sure it is clean, professionally operated and large enough to enable your Bloodhound to exercise.

Training Your
BLOODHOUND

Training a Bloodhound puppy before his hormones 'kick in' will make the job of keeping his attention a thousand-fold easier. The combination of curiosity, sexual urges and that amazing nose can complicate an owner's training lessons.

Living with an untrained dog is a lot like owning a piano that you do not know how to play—it is a nice object to look at, but it does not do much more than that to bring you pleasure. Now try taking piano lessons, and suddenly the piano comes alive and brings forth magical sounds and rhythms that set your heart singing and your body swaying.

The same is true with your Bloodhound. Any dog is a big responsibility and, if not trained sensibly, may develop unacceptable behaviour that annoys you or could even cause family friction.

To train your Bloodhound, you may like to enrol in an obedience class. Teach your dog good manners as you learn how and why he behaves the way he does. Find out how to communicate with your dog and how to recognise and understand his communications with you. More stubborn than your average Beagle, the Bloodhound will never succeed in obedience training the way a Poodle or Labrador Retriever will, but he can be trained to obey the same as any dog.

Those involved with teaching dog obedience and counselling owners about their dogs' behaviour have discovered some interesting facts about dog ownership. For example, training dogs when they are puppies results in the highest rate of success in developing well-mannered and well-adjusted adult dogs. Training an older dog, from six months to six years of age, can produce almost equal results providing that the owner accepts the dog's slower rate of learning capability and is willing to work patiently to help the dog succeed at developing to his fullest potential. Unfortunately, many owners of untrained adult dogs lack the patience factor, so they do not persist until their dogs are successful at learning particular behaviours.

Training a puppy aged 10 to 16 weeks (20 weeks at the most) is like working with a dry sponge in a pool of water. The pup soaks up whatever you show him and constantly looks for more things to do and learn. At this early age, his body is not yet producing hormones, and therein lies the reason for such a high rate of success. Without hormones, he is focused on his owners and not particularly interested in investigating other places, dogs, people, etc. You are his leader: his provider of food, water, shelter and security. He latches onto you and wants to stay close. He will usually follow you from room to room, will not let you out of his sight when you are outdoors with him and will respond in like manner to the people and animals you encounter. If you greet a friend warmly, he will be happy to greet the person as well. If, however, you are hesitant or anxious about the approach of a stranger, he will respond accordingly.

Once the puppy begins to produce hormones, his natural curiosity emerges and he begins to investigate the world around him. It is at this time when you may notice that the untrained dog

begins to wander away from you and even ignore your commands to stay close. When this behaviour becomes a problem, you have two choices: get rid of the dog or train him. It is strongly urged that you choose the latter option.

You usually will be able to find obedience classes within a reasonable distance from your home, but you can also do a lot to train your dog yourself. Sometimes there are classes available, but the tuition is too costly. Whatever the circumstances, the solution to training

The Bloodhound, properly raised and socialised, can make a focused and willing student.

your dog without obedience classes lies within the pages of this book.

This chapter is devoted to helping you train your Bloodhound at home. If the recommended procedures are followed faithfully, you may expect positive results that will prove rewarding both to you and your dog.

Whether your new charge is a puppy or a mature adult, the methods of teaching and the techniques we use in training basic behaviours are the same. After all, no dog, whether puppy or adult, likes harsh or inhumane methods. All creatures, however, respond favourably to gentle motivational methods and sincere praise and encouragement. Now let us get started.

TOILET TRAINING

You can train a puppy to relieve himself wherever you choose, but this must be somewhere suitable. You should bear in mind from the outset that when your puppy is old enough to go out in public places, any canine deposits must be removed at once. You will always have to carry with you a small plastic bag or 'poop-scoop.'

Outdoor training includes such surfaces as grass, hay, soil and cement. Indoor training usually means training your dog to newspaper. When deciding on the surface and location that you

> **TAKE THE LEAD**
>
> Do not carry your dog to his toilet area. Lead him there on a leash or, better yet, encourage him to follow you to the spot. If you start carrying him to his spot, you might end up doing this routine forever and your dog will have the satisfaction of having trained YOU.

will want your Bloodhound to use, be sure it is going to be permanent. Training your dog to grass and then changing your mind a few months later is extremely difficult for both dog and owner.

Next, choose the command you will use each and every time you want your puppy to void. 'Hurry up' and 'Toilet' are examples of commands commonly used by dog owners. Get in the habit of giving the puppy your chosen relief command before you take him out. That way, when he becomes an adult, you will be able to determine if he wants to go out when you ask him. A confirmation will be signs of interest, wagging his tail, watching you intently, going to the door, etc.

Puppy's Needs

Puppy needs to relieve himself after play periods, after each meal, after he has been sleeping and at any time he indicates that he is looking for a place to urinate or defecate. The urinary and intestinal tract muscles of very young puppies are not fully developed. Therefore, like human babies, puppies need to relieve themselves frequently.

Take your puppy out often—every hour for an eight-week-old, for example—and always immediately after sleeping and eating. The older the puppy, the less often he will need to relieve himself. Finally, as a mature healthy adult, he will require only three to five relief trips per day.

Housing

Since the types of housing and control you provide for your puppy have a direct relationship on the success of house-training, we consider the various aspects of both before we begin training.

Taking a new puppy home and turning him loose in your house can be compared to turning a child loose in a sports arena and telling the child that the place is all his! The sheer enormity of the place would be too much for him to handle. Instead, offer the puppy clearly defined areas where he can play, sleep, eat and live. A room of the house where the family gathers is the most obvious choice. Puppies are social animals and need to feel a part of the pack right from the start. Hearing your voice, watching you while you are doing things and smelling you

nearby are all positive reinforcers that he is now a member of your pack. Usually a family room, the kitchen or a nearby adjoining breakfast area is ideal for providing safety and security for both puppy and owner.

Within the designated room, there should be a smaller area that the puppy can call his own. An alcove, a wire or fibreglass dog crate or a fenced (not boarded!) corner from which he can view the activities of his new family will be fine. The size of the area or crate is the key factor here. The area must be large enough so that the puppy can lie down and stretch out, as well as stand up, without rubbing his head on the

The adjustment of living as the sole canine in your human pack will require understanding and encouragement. Your Bloodhound pup spent the first seven to eight weeks of his life snoozing with his brethren under mum's close eye.

CANINE DEVELOPMENT SCHEDULE

It is important to understand how and at what age a puppy develops into adulthood. If you are a puppy owner, consult the following Canine Development Schedule to determine the stage of development your puppy is currently experiencing. This knowledge will help you as you work with the puppy in the weeks and months ahead.

Period	Age	Characteristics
First to Third	Birth to Seven Weeks	Puppy needs food, sleep and warmth, and responds to simple and gentle touching. Needs mother for security and disciplining. Needs littermates for learning and interacting with other dogs. Pup learns to function within a pack and learns pack order of dominance. Begin socialising with adults and children for short periods. Begins to become aware of its environment.
Fourth	Eight to Twelve Weeks	Brain is fully developed. Needs socialising with outside world. Remove from mother and littermates. Needs to change from canine pack to human pack. Human dominance necessary. Fear period occurs between 8 and 12 weeks. Avoid fright and pain.
Fifth	Thirteen to Sixteen Weeks	Training and formal obedience should begin. Less association with other dogs, more with people, places, situations. Period will pass easily if you remember this is pup's change-to-adolescence time. Be firm and fair. Flight instinct prominent. Permissiveness and over-disciplining can do permanent damage. Praise for good behaviour.
Juvenile	Four to Eight Months	Another fear period about 7 to 8 months of age. It passes quickly, but be cautious of fright and pain. Sexual maturity reached. Dominant traits established. Dog should understand sit, down, come and stay by now.

NOTE: THESE ARE APPROXIMATE TIME FRAMES. ALLOW FOR INDIVIDUAL DIFFERENCES IN PUPPIES.

top. At the same time, it must be small enough so that he cannot relieve himself at one end and sleep at the other without coming into contact with his droppings before he is fully trained to relieve himself outside. If you choose to purchase a large crate right away, you can use a divider to confine the pup to the front. Dogs are, by nature, clean animals and will not remain close to their relief areas unless forced to do so. In those cases, they then become dirty dogs and usually remain that way for life.

The dog's designated area should contain clean bedding and a toy. Water must always be available, in a non-spill container.

CONTROL

By control, we mean helping the puppy to create a lifestyle pattern that will be compatible to that of his human pack (YOU!). Just as we guide little children to learn our way of life, we must show the puppy when it is time to play, eat, sleep, exercise and even entertain himself.

Your puppy should always sleep in his crate. He should also learn that, during times of household confusion and excessive human activity, such as at breakfast when family members are preparing for the day, he can play by himself in relative safety and comfort in his designated area. Each time you leave the puppy

HOUSE-TRAINING TIP
Most of all, be consistent. Always take your dog to the same location, always use the same command and always have the dog on lead when he is in his relief area, unless a fenced-in garden is available.

By following the Success Method, your puppy will be completely house-trained by the time his muscle and brain development reach maturity. Keep in mind that small breeds usually mature faster than large breeds, but all puppies should be trained by six months of age.

alone, he should understand exactly where he is to stay.

Puppies are chewers. They cannot tell the difference between lamp cords, television wires, shoes, table legs, etc. Chewing into a television wire, for example, can be fatal to the puppy, while a shorted wire can start a fire in the house. If the puppy chews on the arm of the chair when he is alone, you will probably discipline him angrily when you get home. Thus, he makes the association that your coming home means he is going to be punished. (He will not remember chewing the chair and is incapable of making the association of the discipline with his naughty deed.) Accustoming the pup to his designated area not only keeps him safe but also avoids his engaging in destructive

KEY TO SUCCESS

Success that comes by luck is usually short-lived. Success that comes by well-thought-out proven methods is often more easily achieved and permanent. This is the Success Method. It is designed to give you, the puppy owner, a simple yet proven way to help your puppy develop clean living habits and a feeling of security in his new environment.

THE SUCCESS METHOD

6 Steps to Successful Crate Training

1 Tell the puppy 'Crate time!' and place him in the crate with a small treat (a piece of cheese or half of a biscuit). Let him stay in the crate for five minutes while you are in the same room. Then release him and praise lavishly. Never release him when he is fussing. Wait until he is quiet before you let him out.

2 Repeat Step 1 several times a day.

3 The next day, place the puppy in the crate as before. Let him stay there for ten minutes. Do this several times.

4 Continue building time in five-minute increments until the puppy stays in his crate for 30 minutes with you in the room. Always take him to his relief area after prolonged periods in his crate.

5 Now go back to Step 1 and let the puppy stay in his crate for five minutes, this time while you are out of the room.

6 Once again, build crate time in five-minute increments with you out of the room. When the puppy will stay willingly in his crate (he may even fall asleep!) for 30 minutes with you out of the room, he will be ready to stay in it for several hours at a time.

behaviours when you are not around.

Times of excitement, such as special occasions, family parties, etc., can be fun for the puppy providing that he can view the activities from the security of his designated area. He is not underfoot and he is not being fed all sorts of titbits that will probably cause him stomach distress, yet he still feels a part of the fun.

SCHEDULE

A puppy should be taken to his relief area each time he is released from his designated area, after meals, after a play session and when he first awakens in the morning (at age eight weeks, this can mean 5 a.m.!). The puppy will indicate that he's ready 'to go' by circling or sniffing busily—do not misinterpret these signs. For a puppy less than ten weeks of age, a routine of taking him out every hour is necessary. As the puppy grows, he will be able to wait for longer periods of time.

Keep trips to his relief area short. Stay no more than five or six minutes and then return to the house. If he goes during that time, praise him lavishly and take him indoors immediately. If he does not, but he has an accident when you go back indoors, pick him up immediately, say 'No! No!' and return to his relief area. Wait a few minutes, then return to the house again. Never hit a puppy or rub his face in urine or excrement when he has had an accident!

Once indoors, put the puppy in his crate until you have had time to clean up his accident.

HOW MANY TIMES A DAY?

AGE	RELIEF TRIPS
To 14 weeks	10
14–22 weeks	8
22–32 weeks	6
Adulthood	4
(dog stops growing)	

These are estimates, of course, but they are a guide to the MINIMUM opportunities a dog should have each day to relieve himself.

Then, release him to the family area and watch him more closely than before. Chances are, his accident was a result of your not picking up his signal or waiting too long before offering him the opportunity to relieve himself. Never hold a grudge against the puppy for accidents.

Let the puppy learn that going outdoors means it is time to relieve himself, not to play. Once trained, he will be able to play indoors and out and still differentiate between the times for play versus the times for relief.

Help him develop regular hours for naps, being alone, playing by himself and just resting, all in his crate. Encourage him to entertain himself while you are busy with your activities. Let him learn that having you near is comforting, but it is not your main purpose in life to provide him with undivided attention.

Each time you put your puppy in his own area, use the same command, whatever suits best. Soon he will run to his crate or special area when he hears you say those words.

Crate training provides safety for you, the puppy and the home. It also provides the puppy with a feeling of security, and that helps the puppy achieve self-confidence and clean habits. Remember that one of the primary ingredients in house-training your puppy is

control. Regardless of your lifestyle, there will always be occasions when you will need to have a place where your dog can stay and be happy and safe. Crate training is the answer for now and in the future.

In conclusion, a few key elements are really all you need for a successful house-training method—consistency, frequency, praise, control and supervision. By following these procedures with a normal, healthy puppy, you and the puppy will soon be past the stage of 'accidents' and ready to move on to a full and rewarding life together.

ROLES OF DISCIPLINE, REWARD AND PUNISHMENT

Discipline, training one to act in accordance with rules, brings order to life. It is as simple as that. Without discipline, particularly in a group society, chaos will reign supreme and the group will

TRAINING RULES

If you want to be successful in training your dog, you have four rules to obey yourself:
1. Develop an understanding of how a dog thinks.
2. Do not blame the dog for lack of communication.
3. Define your dog's personality and act accordingly.
4. Have patience and be consistent.

PARENTAL GUIDANCE

Training a dog is a life experience. Many parents admit that much of what they know about raising children they learned from caring for their dogs. Dogs respond to love, fairness and guidance, just as children do. Become a good dog owner and you may become an even better parent.

eventually perish. Humans and canines are social animals and need some form of discipline in order to function effectively. They must procure food, protect their home base and their young and reproduce to keep their species going. If there were no discipline in the lives of social animals, they would eventually die from starvation and/or predation by other stronger animals.

In the case of domestic canines, discipline in their lives is needed in order for them to understand how their pack (you and other family members) functions and how they must act in order to survive.

A large humane society in a highly populated area recently surveyed dog owners regarding their satisfaction with their relationships with their dogs. People who had trained their dogs were 75% more satisfied with their pets than those who had never trained their dogs.

Dr Edward Thorndike, a psychologist, established *Thorndike's Theory of Learning*, which states that a behaviour that results in a pleasant event tends to be repeated. Likewise, a behaviour that results in an unpleasant event tends not to be repeated. It is this theory upon which most training methods are based today. For example, if you manipulate a dog to perform a specific behaviour and reward him for doing it, he is likely to do it again because he enjoyed the end result.

Occasionally, punishment, a penalty inflicted for an offence, is

Although Bloodhounds don't thrive on obedience lessons, they can be attentive students if properly encouraged.

necessary. The best type of punishment often comes from an outside source. For example, a child is told not to touch the stove because he may get burned. He disobeys and touches the stove. In doing so, he receives a burn. From that time on, he respects the heat of the stove and avoids contact with it. Therefore, a behaviour that results in an unpleasant event tends not to be repeated.

A good example of a dog learning the hard way is the dog who chases the house cat. He is told many times to leave the cat alone, yet he persists in teasing the cat. Then, one day, the dog begins chasing the cat but the cat turns and swipes a claw across the dog's face, leaving the dog with a painful gash on his nose. The final result is that the dog stops chasing the cat. Again, a behaviour that results in an unpleasant event tends not to be repeated.

TRAINING EQUIPMENT

COLLAR AND LEAD
For a Bloodhound, the collar and lead that you use for training must be one with which you are easily able to work, not too heavy for the dog and perfectly safe.

TREATS
Have a bag of treats on hand; something nutritious and easy to swallow works best. Use a soft treat, a chunk of cheese or a piece of cooked chicken rather than a dry biscuit. By the time the dog has finished chewing a dry treat, he will forget why he is being rewarded in the first place!

Using food rewards will not teach a dog to beg at the table— the only way to teach a dog to beg at the table is to give him food from the table. In training, rewarding the dog with a food treat will help him associate praise and the treats with learning new behaviours that obviously please his owner.

TRAINING BEGINS: ASK THE DOG A QUESTION
In order to teach your dog anything, you must first get his attention. After all, he cannot learn anything if he is looking away from you with his mind on something else.

To get your dog's attention, ask him 'School?' and immediately walk over to him and give him a treat as you tell him 'Good dog.' Wait a minute or two and repeat the routine, this time with a treat in your hand as you approach within a foot of the dog. Do not go directly to him, but stop about a foot short of him and hold out the treat as you ask 'School?' He will see you approaching with a treat in your hand and most likely begin walking toward you. As you meet, give him the treat and praise again.

The third time, ask the question, have a treat in your hand and walk only a short distance toward the dog so that he must walk almost all the way to you. As he reaches you, give him the treat and praise again.

By this time, the dog will probably be getting the idea that if he pays attention to you, especially when you ask that question, it will pay off in treats and enjoyable activities for him. In other words, he learns that 'school' means doing great things with you that are fun and that result in positive attention for him.

Remember that the dog does not understand your verbal language; he only recognises sounds. Your question translates to a series of sounds for him, and those sounds become the signal to go to you and pay attention. The dog learns that if he does this, he will get to interact with you plus receive treats and praise.

THE BASIC COMMANDS

TEACHING SIT

Now that you have the dog's attention, attach his lead and hold it in your left hand, and hold a food treat in your right hand. Place your food hand at the dog's nose and let him lick the treat but not take it from you. Say 'Sit' and slowly raise your food hand from in front of the dog's nose up over his head so that he is looking at the ceiling. As he bends his head upward, he will have to bend his

Never underestimate the power of a bribe…in canine terminology, that's a food treat. Most Bloodhounds are motivated by an enticing morsel and will quickly learn to obey a command to get a titbit.

knees to maintain his balance. As he bends his knees, he will assume a sit position. At that point, release the food treat and praise lavishly with comments such as 'Good dog! Good sit!,' etc. Remember to always praise enthusiastically, because dogs relish verbal praise from their owners and feel so proud of themselves whenever they accomplish a behaviour.

You will not use food forever in getting the dog to obey your commands. Food is only used to teach new behaviours and, once the dog knows what you want when you give a specific command, you will wean him off the food treats but still maintain the verbal praise. After all, you will always have your voice with you, and there will be many times when you have no food rewards but expect the dog to obey.

TEACHING DOWN

Teaching the down exercise is easy when you understand how the dog perceives the down position, and it is very difficult when you do not. Dogs perceive the down position as a submissive one; therefore, teaching the down exercise by using a forceful method can sometimes make the dog develop such a fear of the down that he either runs away when you say 'Down' or he attempts to snap at the person who tries to force him down.

Have the dog sit close alongside your left leg, facing in the same direction as you are. Hold the lead in your left hand and a food treat in your right. Now place your left hand lightly on the top of the dog's shoulders where they meet above the spinal cord. Do not push down on the dog's shoulders; simply rest your left hand there so you can guide the dog to lie down close to your left leg rather than to swing away from your side when he drops.

Now place the food hand at the dog's nose, say 'Down' very softly (almost a whisper), and slowly lower the food hand to the dog's front feet. When the food hand reaches the floor, begin moving it forward along the floor

Teaching the Bloodhound to sit is an excellent place to start the training sessions. Most dogs respond to the sit command quite readily, especially if a food treat is involved.

in front of the dog. Keep talking softly to the dog, saying things like, 'Do you want this treat? You can do this, good dog.' Your reassuring tone of voice will help calm the dog as he tries to follow the food hand in order to get the treat.

When the dog's elbows touch the floor, release the food and praise softly. Try to get the dog to maintain that down position for several seconds before you let him sit up again. The goal here is to get the dog to settle down and not feel threatened in the down position.

TEACHING STAY

It is easy to teach the dog to stay in either a sit or a down position. Again, we use food and praise during the teaching process as we help the dog to understand exactly what it is that we are expecting him to do.

To teach the sit/stay, start with the dog sitting on your left side as before and hold the lead in your left hand. Have a food treat in your right hand and place your food hand at the dog's nose. Say 'Stay' and step out on your right foot to stand directly in front of the dog, toe to toe, as he licks and nibbles the treat. Be sure to keep his head facing upward to maintain the sit position. Count to five and then swing around to stand next to the dog again with him on your left. As soon as you

DOUBLE JEOPARDY
A dog in jeopardy never lies down. He stays alert on his feet because instinct tells him that he may have to run away or fight for his survival. Therefore, if a dog feels threatened or anxious, he will not lie down. Consequently, it is important to have the dog calm and relaxed as he learns the down exercise.

get back to the original position, release the food and praise lavishly.

To teach the down/stay, do the down as previously described. As soon as the dog lies down, say 'Stay' and step out on your right foot just as you did in the sit/stay. Count to five and then return to stand beside the dog with him on your left side. Release the treat and praise as always.

Within a week or ten days, you can begin to add a bit of distance between you and your dog when you leave him. When

CONSISTENCY PAYS OFF

Dogs need consistency in their feeding schedule, exercise and toilet breaks, and in the verbal commands you use. If you use 'Stay' on Monday and 'Stay here, please' on Tuesday, you will confuse your dog. Don't demand perfect behaviour during training classes and then let him have the run of the house the rest of the day. Above all, lavish praise on your pet consistently every time he does something right. The more he feels he is pleasing you, the more willing he will be to learn.

you do, use your left hand open with the palm facing the dog as a stay signal, much the same as the hand signal a constable uses to stop traffic at an intersection. Hold the food treat in your right hand as before, but this time the food will not be touching the dog's nose. He will watch the food hand and quickly learn that he is going to get that treat as soon as you return to his side.

When you can stand 1 metre away from your dog for 30 seconds, you can then begin building time and distance in both stays. Eventually, the dog can be expected to remain in the stay position for prolonged periods of time until you return to him or call him to you. Always praise lavishly when he stays.

TEACHING COME

If you make teaching 'come' an exciting experience, you should never have a 'student' that does not love the game or that fails to come when called. The secret, it seems, is never to teach the word 'come.'

At times when an owner most wants his dog to come when called, the owner is likely to be upset or anxious and he allows these feelings to come through in the tone of his voice when he calls his dog. Hearing that desperation in his owner's voice, the dog fears the results of going to him and therefore either disobeys outright or runs in the opposite direction. The secret, therefore, is to teach the dog a game and, when you want him to come to you, simply play the game. It is practically a no-fail solution!

To begin, have several members of your family take a few food treats and each go into a different room in the house. Everyone takes turns calling the dog, and each person should celebrate the dog's finding him with a treat and lots of happy praise. When a person calls the dog, he is actually inviting the dog to find him and to get a treat as a reward for 'winning.'

A few turns of the 'Where are you?' game and the dog will understand that everyone is playing the game and that each person has a big celebration awaiting the dog's success at locating him or her. Once the dog learns to love the game, simply calling out 'Where are you?' will bring him running from wherever

he is when he hears that all-important question.

The come command is recognised as one of the most important things to teach a dog, but there are trainers who work with thousands of dogs and never teach the actual word 'Come.' Yet these dogs will race to respond to a person who uses the dog's name followed by 'Where are you?' For example, a woman has a 12-year-old companion dog who went blind, but who never fails to locate her owner when asked, 'Where are you?'

Children, in particular, love to play this game with their dogs. Children can hide in smaller places like a shower or bath, behind a bed or under a table. The dog needs to work a little bit harder to find these hiding places, but, when he does, he loves to celebrate with a treat and a tussle with a favourite youngster.

'COME' . . . BACK

Never call your dog to come to you for a correction or scold him when he reaches you. That is the quickest way to turn a 'Come' command into 'Go away fast!' Dogs think only in the present tense, and your dog will connect the scolding with coming to you, not with the misbehaviour of a few moments earlier.

HEELING WELL

Teach your dog to heel in an enclosed area. Once you think the dog will obey reliably and you want to attempt advanced obedience exercises such as off-lead heeling, test him in a fenced-in area so he cannot run away.

Teaching Heel

Heeling means that the dog walks beside the owner without pulling. It takes time and patience on the owner's part to succeed at teaching the dog that he (the owner) will not proceed unless the dog is walking calmly beside him. Neither pulling out ahead on the lead nor lagging behind is acceptable.

Begin by holding the lead in your left hand as the dog sits beside your left leg. Move the loop end of the lead to your right hand, but keep your left hand short on the lead so that it keeps the dog in close next to you.

Say 'Heel' and step forward on your left foot. Keep the dog close to you and take three steps. Stop and have the dog sit next to you in what we now call the heel position. Praise verbally, but do not touch the dog. Hesitate a moment and begin again with 'Heel,' taking three steps and stopping, at which point the dog is told to sit again.

Your goal here is to have the dog walk those three steps without pulling on the lead. Once he will walk calmly beside you for three steps without pulling, increase the number of steps you take to five. When he will walk politely beside you while you take five steps, you can increase the length of your walk to ten steps. Keep increasing the length of your stroll until the dog will walk quietly beside you without pulling as long as you want him to heel. When you stop heeling, indicate to the dog that the exercise is over by verbally praising as you pet him and say 'OK, good dog.' The 'OK' is used as a release word, meaning that the exercise is finished and the dog is free to relax.

If you are dealing with a dog who insists on pulling you around, simply 'put on your brakes' and stand your ground until the dog realises that the two of you are not going anywhere until he is beside you and moving at your pace, not his. It may take some time just standing there to convince the dog that you are the leader and that you will be the one to decide on the direction and speed of your travel.

Each time the dog looks up at you or slows down to give a slack lead between the two of you, quietly praise him and say, 'Good heel. Good dog.' Eventually, the dog will begin to respond and within a few days he will be walking politely beside you without pulling on the lead. At first, the training sessions should be kept short and very positive; soon the dog will be able to walk nicely with you for increasingly longer distances. Remember also to give the dog free time and the opportunity to run and play when you have finished heel practice.

WEANING OFF FOOD IN TRAINING

Food is used in training new behaviours. Once the dog understands what behaviour goes with a specific command, it is time to start weaning him off the food treats. At first, give a treat after each exercise. Then, start to give a treat only after every other exercise. Mix up the times when you offer a food reward and the times when you only offer praise so that the dog will never know when he is going to receive both food and praise and when he is going to receive only praise. This is called a variable ratio reward system. It proves successful because there is always the chance that the owner will produce a treat, so the dog never stops trying for that reward. No matter what, *always* give verbal praise.

TUG OF WALK?
If you begin teaching the heel by taking long walks and letting the dog pull you along, he misinterprets this action as an acceptable form of taking a walk. When you pull back on the lead to counteract his pulling, he reads that tug as a signal to pull even harder!

OBEDIENCE CLASSES

It is a good idea to enrol in an obedience class if one is available in your area. If yours is a show dog, ringcraft classes would be more appropriate. Many areas have dog clubs that offer basic obedience training as well as preparatory classes for obedience competition. There are also local dog trainers who offer similar classes.

OTHER ACTIVITIES FOR LIFE

Whether a dog is trained in the structured environment of a class or alone with his owner at home, there are many activities that can bring fun and rewards to both owner and dog once they have mastered basic control.

Teaching the dog to help out around the home, in the garden or on the farm provides great satisfaction to both dog and owner. In addition, the dog's help makes life a little easier for his owner and raises his stature as a valued companion to his family. It helps give the dog a purpose by

KEEP SMILING

Never train your dog, puppy or adult, when you are angry or in a sour mood. Dogs are very sensitive to human feelings, especially anger, and if your dog senses that you are angry or upset, he will connect your anger with his training and learn to resent or fear his training sessions.

occupying his mind and providing an outlet for his energy.

Backpacking is an exciting and healthy activity that the dog can be taught without assistance from more than his owner. The exercise of walking and climbing is good for man and dog alike, and the bond that they develop together is priceless. The rule for backpacking with any dog is never to expect the dog to carry more than one-sixth of his body weight.

Not ideal candidates for agility trials, obedience shows or working trials, Bloodhounds are best suited to man-trailing, an

activity that serves their human owners and companions. They do not excel in formal obedience competition, nor are they well suited to any type of hunting today, except in organised events. Basic obedience, as a part of proper acceptable behaviour, is mandatory to maintain reasonable control over such a large and strong-willed animal.

Bloodhounds excel at swimming and can be trained to enter the water on command. Swimming is the perfect exercise for the breed, and puts no strain on its heavy frame.

SAFETY FIRST

While it may seem that the most important things to your dog are eating, sleeping and chewing the upholstery on your furniture, his first concern is actually safety. The domesticated dogs we keep as companions have the same pack instinct as their ancestors who ran free thousands of years ago. Because of this pack instinct, your dog wants to know that he and his pack are not in danger of being harmed, and that his pack has a strong, capable leader. You must establish yourself as the leader early on in your relationship. That way your dog will trust that you will take care of him and the pack, and he will accept your commands without question.

Tally ho! An hunting event befitting the breed's noble heritage... here's the winning pack with its trophy.

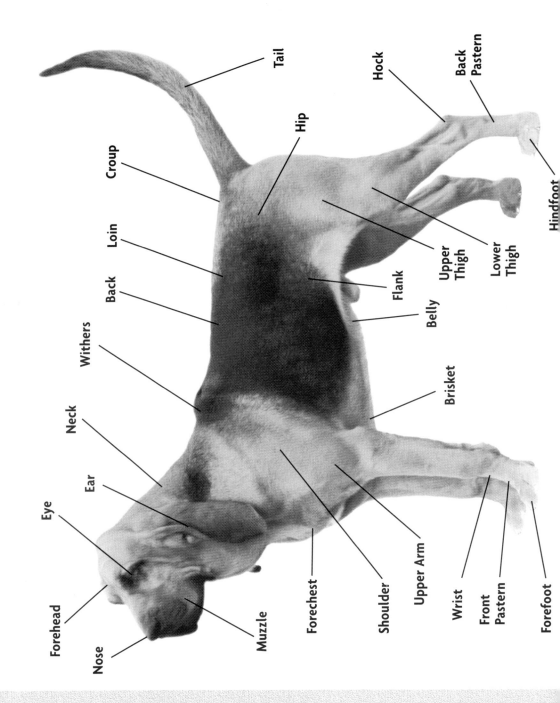

Tail

Hock

Back
Pastern

Hip

Croup

Hindfoot

Loin

Upper
Thigh

Lower
Thigh

Back

Flank

Withers

Belly

Neck

Brisket

Ear

Eye

Forehead

Nose

Muzzle

Forechest

Shoulder

Upper Arm

Wrist

Front
Pastern

Forefoot

PHYSICAL STRUCTURE OF THE BLOODHOUND

Dogs suffer from many of the same physical illnesses as people. They might even share many of the same psychological problems. Since people usually know more about human diseases than canine maladies, many of the terms used in this chapter will be familiar but not necessarily those used by veterinary surgeons. We will use the term *x-ray*, instead of the more acceptable term *radiograph*. We will also use the familiar term *symptoms* even though dogs don't have symptoms, which are verbal descriptions of the patient's feelings; dogs have *clinical signs*. Since dogs can't speak, we have to look for clinical signs...but we still use the term *symptoms* in this book.

As a general rule, medicine is *practised*. That term is not arbitrary. Medicine is a constantly changing art as we learn more and more about genetics, electronic aids (like CAT scans) and daily laboratory advances. There are many dog maladies, like canine hip dysplasia, which are not universally treated in the same manner. Some veterinary surgeons opt for surgery more often than others do.

SELECTING A VETERINARY SURGEON

Your selection of a veterinary surgeon should not be based upon personality (as most are) but upon his convenience to your home. You want a vet who is close because you might have emergencies or need to make multiple visits for treatments. You want a vet who has services that you might require such as tattooing and grooming, as well as sophisticated pet supplies and a good reputation for ability and responsiveness. There is nothing more frustrating than having to wait a day or more to get a response from your veterinary surgeon.

All veterinary surgeons are licensed and their diplomas and/or certificates should be displayed in their waiting rooms. There are, however, many veterinary specialities that usually require further studies and internships. There are specialists in heart problems (veterinary cardiologists), skin problems (veterinary dermatologists), teeth and gum problems (veterinary dentists), eye problems (veterinary ophthalmologists) and x-rays

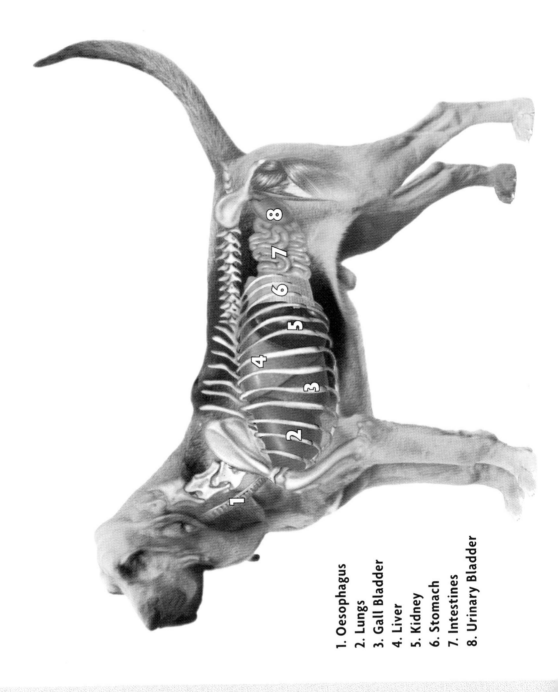

1. Oesophagus
2. Lungs
3. Gall Bladder
4. Liver
5. Kidney
6. Stomach
7. Intestines
8. Urinary Bladder

INTERNAL ORGANS OF THE BLOODHOUND

(veterinary radiologists), as well as vets who have specialities in bones, muscles or other organs. Most veterinary surgeons do routine surgery such as neutering, stitching up wounds and docking tails for those breeds in which such is required for show purposes.

When the problem affecting your dog is serious, it is not unusual or impudent to get another medical opinion, although in Britain you are obliged to advise the vets concerned about this. You might also want to compare costs among several veterinary surgeons. Sophisticated health care and veterinary services can be very costly. It is not infrequent that important decisions are based upon financial considerations.

PREVENTATIVE MEDICINE

It is much easier, less costly and more effective to practise preventative medicine than to fight bouts of illness and disease. Properly bred puppies come from parents who were selected based upon their genetic disease profiles. Their mothers should have been vaccinated, free of all internal and external parasites and properly nourished. The dam can pass on disease resistance to her puppies, which can last for eight to ten weeks, but she can also pass on parasites and many infections. For these reasons, a

Breakdown of Veterinary Income by Category

2%	Dentistry
4%	Radiology
12%	Surgery
15%	Vaccinations
19%	Laboratory
23%	Examinations
25%	Medicines

A typical American vet's income, categorised according to services performed. This survey dealt with small-animal (pets) practices.

visit to the veterinary surgeon who cared for the dam is recommended.

VACCINATION SCHEDULING

Most vaccinations are given by injection and should only be done by a veterinary surgeon. Both he and you should keep records of the date of the injection, the identification of the vaccine and the amount given. Some vets give a first vaccination at eight weeks, but most dog breeders prefer the course not to commence until about ten weeks to avoid negating any antibodies passed on by the dam. The vaccination scheduling is usually based on a 15-day cycle. You must take your vet's advice regarding when to vaccinate, as this may differ according to the vaccine used. Most vaccinations immunize your puppy against viruses.

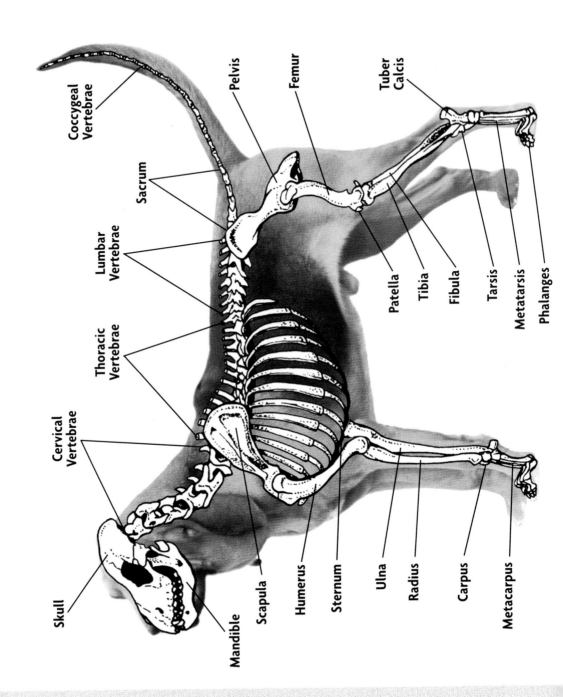

Coccygeal Vertebrae

Pelvis

Femur

Tuber Calcis

Sacrum

Lumbar Vertebrae

Thoracic Vertebrae

Cervical Vertebrae

Patella

Tibia

Fibula

Tarsis

Metatarsis

Phalanges

Skull

Mandible

Scapula

Humerus

Sternum

Ulna

Radius

Carpus

Metacarpus

SKELETAL STRUCTURE OF THE BLOODHOUND

The usual vaccines contain immunizing doses of several different viruses such as distemper, parvovirus, parain-fluenza and hepatitis, although some veterinary surgeons recommend separate vaccines for each disease. There are other vaccines available when the puppy is at risk. You should rely upon professional advice. This is especially true for the booster-shot programme. Most vaccina-tion programmes require a booster when the puppy is a year old and once a year thereafter. In some cases, circumstances may require more or less frequent immunizations.

Kennel cough, more formally known as tracheobronchitis, is treated with a vaccine that is sprayed into the dog's nostrils. Kennel cough is usually included in routine vaccination, but this is often not so effective as for other major diseases.

WEANING TO FIVE MONTHS OLD
Puppies should be weaned by the time they are about two months old. A puppy that remains for at least eight weeks with its mother and littermates usually adapts better to other dogs and people later in life. Some new owners have their puppies examined by veterinary surgeons immediately, which is a good idea. Vaccination programmes usually begin when the puppy is very young.

The puppy will have its teeth examined, and have its skeletal conformation and general health checked prior to certification by the veterinary surgeon. Puppies in certain breeds may have problems with their kneecaps, cataracts and other eye problems, heart murmurs or undescended testicles. They may also have personality problems, and your veterinary surgeon might have training in temperament evalua-tion.

FIVE TO TWELVE MONTHS OF AGE
Unless you intend to breed or show your dog, neutering the puppy at six months of age is recommended. Discuss this with your veterinary surgeon. Neutering has proven to be extremely beneficial to both male and female puppies. Besides eliminating the possibility of pregnancy, it inhibits (but does not prevent) breast cancer in bitches and prostate cancer in male dogs. Under no circum-stances should a bitch be spayed prior to her first season.

Your veterinary surgeon should provide your puppy with a thorough dental evaluation at six months of age, ascertaining whether all the permanent teeth have erupted properly. A home dental care regimen should be initiated at six months, including brushing weekly and providing good dental devices (such as nylon bones). Regular dental care promotes healthy teeth, fresh breath and a longer life.

ONE TO SIX YEARS

Once a year, your grown dog should visit the vet for an examination and vaccination boosters, if needed. Some vets recommend blood tests, a thyroid level check and a dental evaluation to accompany these annual visits. A thorough clinical evaluation by the vet can provide critical background information for your dog. Blood tests are often performed at one year of age, and dental examinations around the third birthday. In the long run, quality preventative care for your pet can save money, teeth and lives.

SKIN PROBLEMS IN BLOODHOUNDS

Veterinary surgeons are consulted by dog owners for skin problems more than for any other group of diseases or maladies, and the Bloodhound is no exception given its pendulous excessive skin. The Bloodhound's skin is almost as sensitive as human skin, and both suffer from almost the same ailments (though the occurrence of acne in dogs is rare). For this reason, veterinary dermatology has developed into a speciality practised by many veterinary surgeons.

Since many skin problems have visual symptoms that are almost identical, it requires the skill of an experienced veterinary dermatologist to identify and cure many of the more severe skin disorders. Pet shops sell many treatments for skin problems, but most of the treatments are directed at the symptoms and not the underlying problem(s). If your dog is suffering from a skin disorder, you should seek professional assistance as quickly as possible. As with all diseases, the earlier a problem is identified and treated, the more successful is the cure.

HEREDITARY SKIN DISORDERS

Veterinary dermatologists are currently researching a number of skin disorders that are believed to have an hereditary basis. These inherited diseases are transmitted by both parents, who appear (phenotypically) normal but have a recessive gene for the disease, meaning that they carry, but are not affected by, the disease. These diseases pose serious problems to breeders because in some instances there are no methods of identifying carriers. Often the secondary diseases associated with these skin conditions are even more debilitating than the skin disorders themselves, including cancers and respiratory problems; others can be lethal.

Among the hereditary skin disorders, for which the mode of inheritance is known, are: acrodermatitis, cutaneous asthenia (Ehlers-Danlos syndrome), sebaceous adenitis, cyclic hematopoiesis, dermatomyositis, IgA deficiency, colour dilution alopaecia and nodular dermatofibrosis. Some of these disorders are limited to one or two breeds, while others affect a large number of breeds. All inherited diseases must be diagnosed and treated by a veterinary specialist.

PARASITE BITES

Many of us are allergic to insect bites. The bites itch, erupt and may even become infected. Dogs have the same reaction to fleas,

Skin problems are common in all breeds, and the Bloodhound is, unfortunately, no exception. If your pup is continually licking at an area, it is wise to have the vet give it a look.

HEALTH AND VACCINATION SCHEDULE

Age in Weeks:	6th	8th	10th	12th	14th	16th	20-24th	52nd
Worm Control	✔	✔	✔	✔	✔	✔	✔	
Neutering								✔
Heartworm		✔		✔		✔	✔	
Parvovirus	✔		✔		✔		✔	✔
Distemper		✔		✔		✔		✔
Hepatitis		✔		✔		✔		✔
Leptospirosis								✔
Parainfluenza	✔		✔		✔			✔
Dental Examination		✔					✔	✔
Complete Physical		✔					✔	✔
Coronavirus				✔			✔	✔
Kennel Cough	✔							
Hip Dysplasia								✔
Rabies							✔	

Vaccinations are not instantly effective. It takes about two weeks for the dog's immune system to develop antibodies. Most vaccinations require annual booster shots. Your veterinary surgeon should guide you in this regard.

ticks and/or mites. When an insect lands on you, you have the chance to whisk it away with your hand. Unfortunately, when your dog is bitten by a flea, tick or mite, he can only scratch it away or bite it. By the time the dog has been bitten, the parasite has done some of its damage. It may also have laid eggs, which will cause further problems in the near future. The itching from parasite bites is probably due to the saliva injected into the site when the parasite sucks the dog's blood.

Auto-Immune Skin Conditions

An auto-immune skin condition is commonly referred to as a condition in which a person (or dog) is 'allergic' to him- or herself, while an allergy is usually an inflammatory reaction to an outside stimulus. Auto-immune diseases cause serious damage to the tissues that are involved.

The best known auto-immune disease is lupus, which affects people as well as dogs. The symptoms are variable and may affect the kidneys, bones, blood chemistry and skin. It can be fatal to both dogs and humans, though it is not thought to be transmissible. It is usually successfully treated with cortisone, prednisone or a similar corticosteroid, but extensive use of these drugs can have harmful side effects.

ACRAL LICK GRANULOMA
Many large dogs have a very poorly understood syndrome called acral lick granuloma. The manifestation of the problem is the dog's tireless attack at a specific area of the body, almost always the legs or paws. The dog

SIMULATED MEDICAL CONDITION FOR EDUCATIONAL PURPOSES ONLY.

An acral lick granuloma develops when the Bloodhound attacks a particular spot incessantly until it is raw and bleeding. Usually on his leg or paw, the syndrome can occur in a variety of locations.

DISEASE REFERENCE CHART

	What is it?	What causes it?	Symptoms
Leptospirosis	Severe disease that affects the internal organs; can be spread to people.	A bacterium, which is often carried by rodents, that enters through mucous membranes and spreads quickly throughout the body.	Range from fever, vomiting and loss of appetite in less severe cases to shock, irreversible kidney damage and possibly death in most severe cases.
Rabies	Potentially deadly virus that infects warm-blooded mammals. Not seen in United Kingdom.	Bite from a carrier of the virus, mainly wild animals.	1st stage: dog exhibits change in behaviour, fear. 2nd stage: dog's behaviour becomes more aggressive. 3rd stage: loss of coordination, trouble with bodily functions.
Parvovirus	Highly contagious virus, potentially deadly.	Ingestion of the virus, which is usually spread through the faeces of infected dogs.	Most common: severe diarrhoea. Also vomiting, fatigue, lack of appetite.
Kennel cough	Contagious respiratory infection.	Combination of types of bacteria and virus. Most common: *Bordetella bronchiseptica* bacteria and parainfluenza virus.	Chronic cough.
Distemper	Disease primarily affecting respiratory and nervous system.	Virus that is related to the human measles virus.	Mild symptoms such as fever, lack of appetite and mucous secretion progress to evidence of brain damage, 'hard pad.'
Hepatitis	Virus primarily affecting the liver.	Canine adenovirus type I (CAV-1). Enters system when dog breathes in particles.	Lesser symptoms include listlessness, diarrhoea, vomiting. More severe symptoms include 'blue-eye' (clumps of virus in eye).
Coronavirus	Virus resulting in digestive problems.	Virus is spread through infected dog's faeces.	Stomach upset evidenced by lack of appetite, vomiting, diarrhoea.

licks so intensively that he removes the hair and skin, leaving an ugly, large wound. Tiny protuberances, which are outgrowths of new capillaries, bead on the surface of the wound. Owners who notice their dogs' biting and chewing at their extremities should have the vet determine the cause. If lick granuloma is identified, although there is no absolute cure, corticosteroids are the most common treatment.

AIRBORNE ALLERGIES

An interesting allergy is pollen allergy. Humans have hay fever, rose fever and other fevers from which they suffer during the pollinating season. Many dogs suffer the same allergies. When the pollen count is high, your dog might suffer, but don't expect him to sneeze and have a runny nose as a human would. Dogs react to pollen allergies the same way they react to fleas—they scratch and bite themselves.

Dogs, like humans, can be tested for allergens. Discuss the testing with your veterinary dermatologist.

FOOD PROBLEMS

FOOD ALLERGIES

Dogs are allergic to many foods that are best-sellers and highly recommended by breeders and veterinary surgeons. Changing the brand of food that you buy may not eliminate the problem if the element to which the dog is allergic is contained in the new brand.

Recognising a food allergy is difficult. Humans vomit or have rashes when they eat a food to which they are allergic. Dogs neither vomit nor (usually) develop rashes. They react in the same manner as they would to an airborne or flea allergy: they itch, scratch and bite, thus making the diagnosis extremely difficult. While pollen allergies and parasite bites are usually seasonal, food allergies are year-round problems.

FOOD INTOLERANCE

Food intolerance is the inability of the dog to completely digest certain foods. For instance, puppies that may have done very well on their mother's milk may not do well on cow's milk. The results of food intolerance may be evident in loose bowels, passing gas and stomach pains. These are the only obvious symptoms of food intolerance, which makes diagnosis difficult.

TREATING FOOD PROBLEMS

It is possible to handle food allergies and food intolerance yourself. Start by putting your dog on a diet that he has never had. Obviously, if the dog has never eaten this new food, he can't have been allergic or intolerant of it. Start with a single ingredient that is not in the dog's diet at the present time. Ingredients like chopped beef or fish are common in dogs' diets, so try something more exotic like rabbit, pheasant or even just vegetables. Keep the dog on this diet (with no additives) for a month. If the symptoms of food allergy or intolerance disappear, it is quite likely that your dog has a food allergy.

Don't think that the single ingredient cured the problem. You still must find a suitable diet and ascertain which ingredient in the old diet was objectionable. This is most easily done by adding ingredients to the new diet one at a time. Let the dog stay on the modified diet for a month before you add another ingredient. Eventually, you will determine the ingredient that caused the adverse reaction.

An alternative method is to carefully study the ingredients in the diet to which your dog is allergic or intolerant. Identify the main ingredient in this diet and eliminate the main ingredient by buying a different food that does not have that ingredient. Keep experimenting until the symptoms disappear after one month on the new diet.

Puppies and adults alike can develop allergies related to their environment. Carefully consider the various plants and bushes to which your Bloodhound has access.

EXTERNAL PARASITES

FLEAS

Of all the problems to which dogs are prone, none is more well known and frustrating than fleas. Flea infestation is relatively simple to cure but difficult to prevent. Parasites that are harboured inside the body are a bit more difficult to eradicate but they are easier to control.

Magnified head of a dog flea, *Ctenocephalides canis.*

S. E. M. BY DR DENNIS KUNKEL, UNIVERSITY OF HAWAII

To control flea infestation, you have to understand the flea's life cycle. Fleas are often thought of as a summertime problem, but centrally heated homes have changed the patterns and fleas can be found at any time of the year. The most effective method of flea control is a two-stage approach: one stage to kill the adult fleas, and the other to control the development of pre-adult fleas. Unfortunately, no single active ingredient is effective against all stages of the life cycle.

LIFE CYCLE STAGES

During its life, a flea will pass through four life stages: egg, larva, pupa and adult. The adult stage is the most visible and irritating stage of the flea life cycle, and this is

Opposite page: A scanning electron micrograph of a dog or cat flea, *Ctenocephalides,* magnified more than 100x. This image has been colorized for effect.

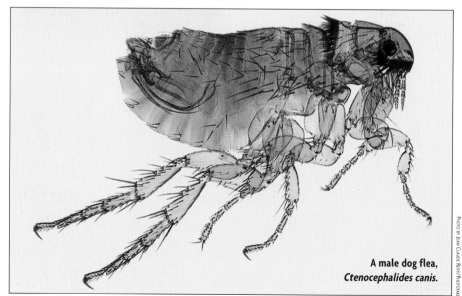

PHOTO BY JEAN CLAUDE REVY/PHOTOTAKE

A male dog flea, *Ctenocephalides canis.*

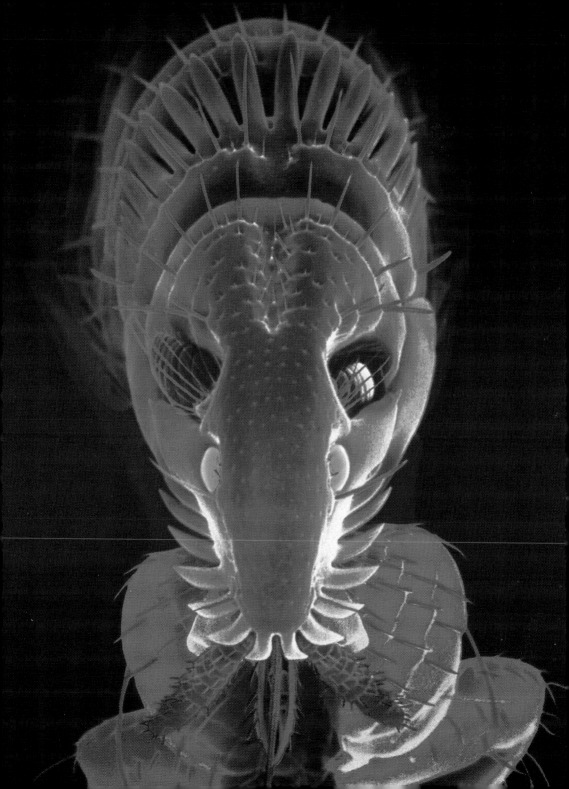

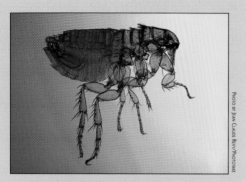

Photo by Jean Claude Revy/Phototake

A LOOK AT FLEAS

Fleas have been around for millions of years and have adapted to changing host animals. They are able to go through a complete life cycle in less than one month or they can extend their lives to almost two years by remaining as pupae or cocoons. They do not need blood or any other food for up to 20 months.

They have been measured as being able to jump 300,000 times and can jump 150 times their length in any direction, including straight up. Those are just a few of the reasons why they are so successful in infesting a dog!

why the majority of flea-control products concentrate on this stage. The fact is that adult fleas account for only 1% of the total flea population, and the other 99% exist in pre-adult stages, i.e. eggs, larvae and pupae. The pre-adult stages are barely visible to the naked eye.

THE LIFE CYCLE OF THE FLEA

Eggs are laid on the dog, usually in quantities of about 20 or 30, several times a day. The female adult flea must have a blood meal before each egg-laying session. When first laid, the eggs will cling to the dog's hair, as the eggs are still moist. However, they will quickly dry out and fall from the dog, especially if the dog moves around or scratches. Many eggs will fall off in the dog's favourite area or an area in which he spends a lot of time, such as his bed.

Once the eggs fall from the dog onto the carpet or furniture, they will hatch into larvae. This takes from one to ten days. Larvae are not particularly mobile and will usually travel only a few inches

The Life Cycle of the Flea

Eggs

Larvae

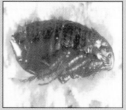

Pupa

Adult

Photos courtesy of Fleabusters®/Rx for Fleas.

FLEA KILLERS

Flea-killers are poisonous. You should not spray these toxic chemicals on areas of a dog's body that he licks, on his genitals or on his face. Flea killers taken internally are a better answer, but check with your vet in case internal therapy is not advised for your dog.

INSECT GROWTH REGULATOR (IGR)

Two types of products should be used when treating fleas—a product to treat the pet and a product to treat the home. Adult fleas represent less than 1% of the flea population. The pre-adult fleas (eggs, larvae and pupae) represent more than 99% of the flea population and are found in the environment; it is in the case of pre-adult fleas that products containing an Insect Growth Regulator (IGR) should be used in the home.

IGRs are a new class of compounds used to prevent the development of insects. They do not kill the insect outright, but instead use the insect's biology against it to stop it from completing its growth. Products that contain methoprene are the world's first and leading IGRs. Used to control fleas and other insects, this type of IGR will stop flea larvae from developing and protect the house for up to seven months.

from where they hatch. However, they do have a tendency to move away from light and heavy traffic—under furniture and behind doors are common places to find high quantities of flea larvae.

The flea larvae feed on dead organic matter, including adult flea faeces, until they are ready to change into adult fleas. Fleas will usually remain as larvae for around seven days. After this period, the larvae will pupate into protective pupae. While inside the pupae, the larvae will undergo metamorphosis and change into adult fleas. This can take as little time as a few days, but the adult fleas can remain inside the pupae waiting to hatch for up to two years. The pupae are signalled to hatch by certain stimuli, such as physical pressure—the pupae's being stepped on, heat from an animal's lying on the pupae or increased carbon dioxide levels and vibrations—indicating that a suitable host is available.

Once hatched, the adult flea must feed within a few days. Once the adult flea finds a host, it will not leave voluntarily. It only becomes dislodged by grooming or the host animal's scratching. The adult flea will remain on the host for the duration of its life unless forcibly removed.

Photo by Dwight R Kuhn

Dwight R Kuhn's magnificent action photo, showing a flea jumping from a dog's back.

TREATING THE ENVIRONMENT AND THE DOG

Treating fleas should be a two-pronged attack. First, the environment needs to be treated; this includes carpets and furniture, especially the dog's bedding and areas underneath furniture. The environment should be treated with a household spray containing an Insect Growth Regulator (IGR) and an insecticide to kill the adult fleas. Most IGRs are effective against eggs and larvae; they

EN GARDE: CATCHING FLEAS OFF GUARD!
Consider the following ways to arm yourself against fleas:
• Add a small amount of pennyroyal or eucalyptus oil to your dog's bath. These natural remedies repel fleas.
• Supplement your dog's food with fresh garlic (minced or grated) and a hearty amount of brewer's yeast, both of which ward off fleas.
• Use a flea comb on your dog daily. Submerge fleas in a cup of bleach to kill them quickly.
• Confine the dog to only a few rooms to limit the spread of fleas in the home.
• Vacuum daily...and get all of the crevices! Dispose of the bag every few days until the problem is under control.
• Wash your dog's bedding daily. Cover cushions where your dog sleeps with towels, and wash the towels often.

A scanning electron micrograph (S. E. M.) of a dog flea, *Ctenocephalides canis.*

S. E. M. by Dr Dennis Kunkel, University of Hawaii

actually mimic the fleas' own hormones and stop the eggs and larvae from developing into adult fleas. There are currently no treatments available to attack the pupa stage of the life cycle, so the adult insecticide is used to kill the newly hatched adult fleas before they find a host. Most IGRs are active for many months, while adult insecticides are only active for a few days.

When treating with a household spray, it is a good idea to vacuum before applying the product. This stimulates as many pupae as possible to hatch into adult fleas. The vacuum cleaner should also be treated with an insecticide to prevent the eggs and larvae that have been hoovered into the vacuum bag from hatching.

The second stage of treatment is to apply an adult insecticide to the dog. Traditionally, this would be in the form of a collar or a spray, but more recent innovations include digestible insecticides that poison the fleas when they ingest the dog's blood. Alternatively, there are drops that, when placed on the back of the animal's neck, spread throughout the fur and skin to kill adult fleas.

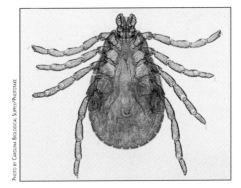

A brown dog tick, *Rhipicephalus sanguineus*, is an uncommon but annoying tick found on dogs.

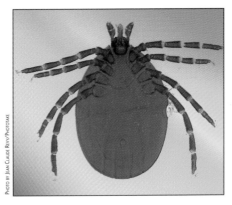

An uncommon dog tick of the genus *Ixode*. Magnified 10x.

TICKS AND MITES

Though not as common as fleas, ticks and mites are found all over the tropical and temperate world. They don't bite, like fleas; they harpoon. They dig their sharp proboscis (nose) into the dog's skin and drink the blood. Their only food and drink is dog's blood. Dogs can get Lyme disease, Rocky Mountain spotted fever (normally found in the US only), paralysis and many other diseases from ticks and mites. They may live where fleas are

The head of a dog tick, *Dermacentor variabilis*, enlarged and coloured for effect.

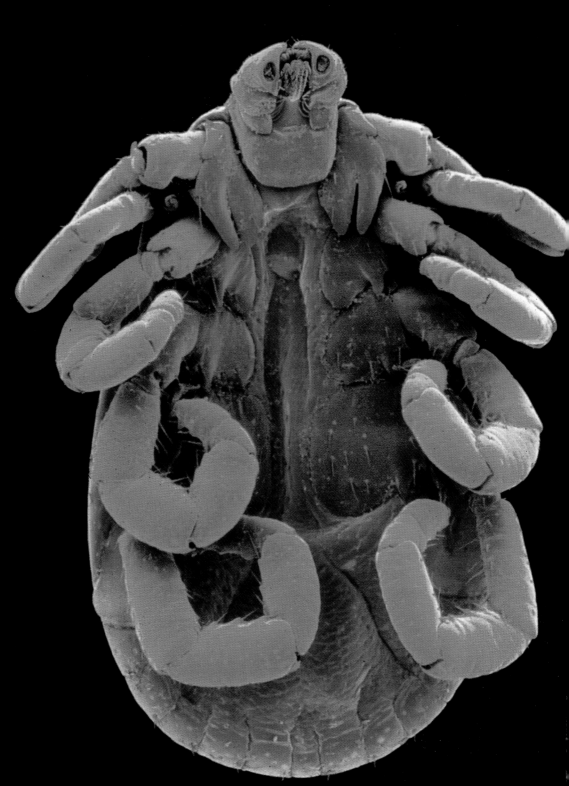

Human lice look like dog lice and
the two are closely related.

BEWARE THE DEER TICK

The great outdoors may be fun for your dog, but it also is a home to dangerous ticks. Deer ticks carry a bacterium known as *Borrelia burgdorferi* and are most active in the autumn and spring. When infections are caught early, penicillin and tetracycline are effective antibiotics, but if left untreated, the bacteria may cause neurological, kidney and cardiac problems as well as long-term trouble with walking and painful joints.

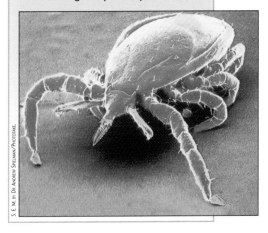

found and they like to hide in cracks or seams in walls wherever dogs live. They are controlled the same way fleas are controlled.

The dog tick, *Dermacentor variabilis*, may well be the most common dog tick in many geographical areas, especially those areas where the climate is hot and humid.

Most dog ticks have life expectancies of a week to six months, depending upon climatic conditions. They can neither jump nor fly, but they

Opposite page:
The dog tick, *Dermacentor variabilis*, is probably the most common tick found on dogs. Look at the strength in its eight legs! No wonder it's hard to detach them.

can crawl slowly and can range up to 5 metres (16 feet) to reach a sleeping or unsuspecting dog.

MANGE

Mites cause a skin irritation called mange. Some are contagious, like *Cheyletiella*, ear mites, scabies and chiggers. Mites that cause ear-mite infestations are usually controlled with Lindane, which can only be

The mange mite, *Psoroptes bovis*.

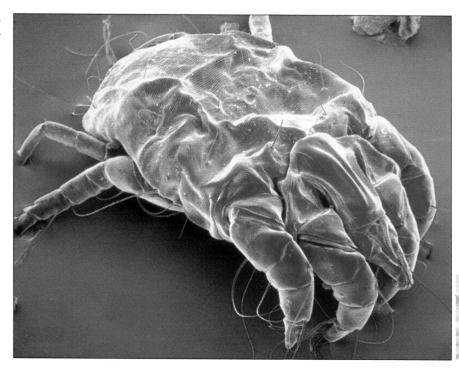

The roundworm, *Rhabditis*. The roundworm can infect both dogs and humans.

PHOTO BY CAROLINA BIOLOGICAL SUPPLY/PHOTOTAKE

The common roundworm, *Ascaris lumbricoides*.

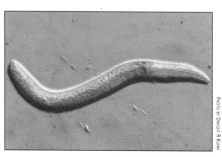

PHOTO BY DWIGHT R KUHN

administered by a vet, followed by Tresaderm at home.

It is essential that your dog be treated for mange as quickly as possible because some forms of mange are transmissible to people.

INTERNAL PARASITES

Most animals—fishes, birds and mammals, including dogs and humans—have worms and other parasites that live inside their bodies. According to Dr Herbert R Axelrod, the fish pathologist, there are two kinds of parasites: dumb and smart. The smart parasites live in peaceful cooperation with their hosts (symbiosis), while the dumb parasites kill their hosts. Most of the worm infections are relatively easy to control. If they are not controlled, they weaken the host dog to the point that other medical problems occur, but they are not dumb parasites.

ROUNDWORMS

The roundworms that infect dogs are scientifically known as *Toxocara canis*. They live in the dog's intestines. The worms shed eggs continually. It has been estimated that a dog produces about 150 grammes of faeces every day. Each gramme of faeces

ROUNDWORMS

Average size dogs can pass 1,360,000 roundworm eggs every day. For example, if there were only 1 million dogs in the world, the world would be saturated with 1,300 metric tonnes of dog faeces. These faeces would contain 15,000,000,000 roundworm eggs.

Up to 31% of home gardens and children's play boxes in the US contain roundworm eggs.

Flushing dog's faeces down the toilet is not a safe practice because the usual sewage treatments do not destroy roundworm eggs.

Infected puppies start shedding roundworm eggs at 3 weeks of age. They can be infected by their mother's milk.

DEWORMING

Ridding your puppy of worms is *very important* because certain worms that puppies carry, such as tapeworms and roundworms, can infect humans.

Breeders initiate deworming programmes at or about four weeks of age. The routine is repeated every two or three weeks until the puppy is three months old. The breeder from whom you obtained your puppy should provide you with the complete details of the deworming programme.

Your veterinary surgeon can prescribe and monitor the programme of deworming for you. The usual programme is treating the puppy every 15–20 days until the puppy is positively worm-free. It is advised that you only treat your puppy with drugs that are recommended professionally.

averages 10,000–12,000 eggs of roundworms. There are no known areas in which dogs roam that do not contain roundworm eggs. The greatest danger of roundworms is that they infect people too! It is wise to have your dog tested regularly for roundworms.

Pigs also have roundworm infections that can be passed to humans and dogs. The typical roundworm parasite is called *Ascaris lumbricoides*.

Left: The roundworm *Rhabditis*. Right: Male and female hookworms. *Ancylostoma caninum* are uncommonly found in pet or show dogs in Britain.

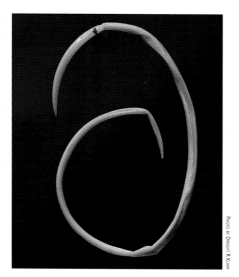

PHOTO BY DWIGHT R KUHN

PHOTO BY DWIGHT R KUHN

HOOKWORMS

The worm *Ancylostoma caninum* is commonly called the dog hookworm. It is also dangerous to humans and cats. It has teeth by which it attaches itself to the intestines of the dog. It changes the site of its attachment about six times a day and the dog loses blood from each detachment, possibly causing iron-deficiency anaemia. Hookworms are easily purged from the dog with many medications. Milbemycin oxime, which also serves as a heartworm preventative in Collies, can be used for this purpose.

In Britain the 'temperate climate' hookworm (*Uncinaria stenocephala*) is rarely found in pet or show dogs, but can occur in hunting packs, racing Greyhounds and sheepdogs because the worms can be prevalent wherever dogs are exercised regularly on grassland.

TAPEWORMS

There are many species of tapeworm. They are carried by fleas! The dog eats the flea and starts the tapeworm cycle. Humans can also be infected with tapeworms, so don't eat fleas! Fleas are so small that your dog could pass them onto your hands, your plate or your food and thus make it possible for you to ingest a flea that is carrying tapeworm eggs.

The infective stage of the hookworm larva.

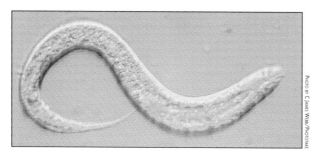

PHOTO BY C JAMES WEBB/PHOTOTAKE

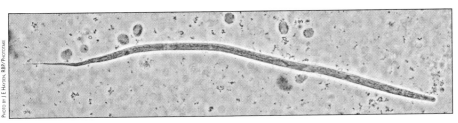

Heartworm, *Dirofilaria immitis.*

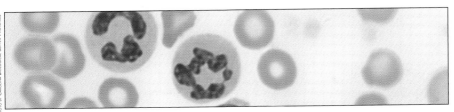

Magnified heartworm larvae, *Dirofilaria immitis.*

While tapeworm infection is not life-threatening in dogs (smart parasite!), it can be the cause of a very serious liver disease for humans. About 50 percent of the humans infected with *Echinococcus multilocularis*, a type of tapeworm that causes alveolar hydatis, perish.

TAPEWORMS

Humans, rats, squirrels, foxes, coyotes, wolves and domestic dogs are all susceptible to tapeworm infection. Except in humans, tapeworms are usually not a fatal infection. Infected individuals can harbour a thousand parasitic worms.

Tapeworms have two sexes—male and female (many other worms have only one sex—male and female in the same worm).

If dogs eat infected rats or mice, they get the tapeworm disease. One month after attaching to a dog's intestine, the worm starts shedding eggs. These eggs are infective immediately. Infective eggs can live for a few months without a host animal.

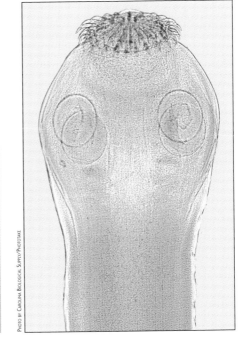

The head and rostellum (the round prominence on the scolex) of a tapeworm, which infects dogs and humans.

The heart of a dog infected with canine heartworm, *Dirofilaria immitis.*

PHOTO BY JAMES E HAYDEN, RPB/PHOTOTAKE

HEARTWORMS

Heartworms are thin, extended worms up to 30 cms (12 ins) long, which live in a dog's heart and the major blood vessels surrounding it. Dogs may have up to 200 worms. Symptoms may be loss of energy, loss of appetite, coughing, the development of a pot belly and anaemia.

Heartworms are transmitted by mosquitoes. The mosquito drinks the blood of an infected dog and takes in larvae with the blood. The larvae, called microfilaria, develop within the body of the mosquito and are passed on to the next dog bitten after the larvae mature. It takes two to three weeks for the larvae to develop to the infective stage within the body of the mosquito. Dogs should be treated at about six weeks of age, and maintained on a prophylactic dose given monthly.

Blood testing for heartworms is not necessarily indicative of how seriously your dog is infected. This is a dangerous disease. Although heartworm is a problem for dogs in America, Australia, Asia and Central Europe, dogs in the United Kingdom are not currently affected by heartworm.

First Aid at a Glance

Burns
Place the affected area under cool water; use ice if only a small area is burnt.

Bee/Insect bites
Apply ice to relieve swelling; antihistamine dosed properly.

Animal bites
Clean any bleeding area; apply pressure until bleeding subsides; go to the vet.

Spider bites
Use cold compress and a pressurised pack to inhibit venom's spreading.

Antifreeze poisoning
Induce vomiting with hydrogen peroxide. Seek *immediate* veterinary help!

Fish hooks
Removal best handled by vet; hook must be cut in order to remove.

Snake bites
Pack ice around bite; contact vet quickly; identify snake for proper antivenin.

Car accident
Move dog from roadway with blanket; seek veterinary aid.

Shock
Calm the dog, keep him warm; seek immediate veterinary help.

Nosebleed
Apply cold compress to the nose; apply pressure to any visible abrasion.

Bleeding
Apply pressure above the area; treat wound by applying a cotton pack.

Heat stroke
Submerge dog in cold bath; cool down with fresh air and water; go to the vet.

Frostbite/Hypothermia
Warm the dog with a warm bath, electric blankets or hot water bottles.

Abrasions
Clean the wound and wash out thoroughly with fresh water; apply antiseptic.

 Remember: an injured dog may attempt to bite a helping hand from fear and confusion. Always muzzle the dog before trying to offer assistance.

HOMEOPATHY:
an alternative to conventional medicine

'Less is Most'

Using this principle, the strength of a homeopathic remedy is measured by the number of serial dilutions that were undertaken to create it. The greater the number of serial dilutions, the greater the strength of the homeopathic remedy. The potency of a remedy that has been made by making a dilution of 1 part in 100 parts (or 1/100) is 1c or 1cH. If this remedy is subjected to a series of further dilutions, each one being 1/100, a more dilute and stronger remedy is produced. If the remedy is diluted in this way six times, it is called 6c or 6cH. A dilution of 6c is 1 part in 1,000,000,000,000. In general, higher potencies in more frequent doses are better for acute symptoms and lower potencies in more infrequent doses are more useful for chronic, long-standing problems.

CURING OUR DOGS NATURALLY

Holistic medicine means treating the whole animal as a unique, perfect living being. Generally, holistic treatments do not suppress the symptoms that the body naturally produces, as do most medications prescribed by conventional doctors and vets. Holistic methods seek to cure disease by regaining balance and harmony in the patient's environment. Some of these methods include use of nutritional therapy, herbs, flower essences, aromatherapy, acupuncture, massage, chiropractic and, of course, the most popular holistic approach, homeopathy.

Homeopathy is a theory or system of treating illness with small doses of substances which, if administered in larger quantities, would produce the symptoms that the patient already has. This approach is often described as 'like cures like.' Although modern veterinary medicine is geared toward the 'quick fix,' homeopathy relies on the belief that, given the time, the body is able to heal itself and return to its natural, healthy state.

Choosing a remedy to cure a problem in our dogs is the difficult part of homeopathy. Consult with your veterinary surgeon for a professional diagnosis of your dog's symptoms. Often these symptoms require immediate conventional care. If your vet is willing, and knowledgeable, you may attempt a homeopathic remedy. Be aware that cortisone prevents homeopathic remedies from working. There are hundreds of possibilities and combinations to cure many problems in dogs, from basic physical problems such as excessive moulting, fleas, obesity or other parasites, unattractive doggy odour, bad breath, upset tummy,

dry, oily or dull coat, diarrhoea, ear problems or eye discharge (including tears and dry or mucousy matter), to behavioural abnormalities, such as fear of loud noises, habitual licking, poor appetite, excessive barking, and various phobias. From alumina to zincum metallicum, the remedies span the planet and the imagination...from flowers and weeds to chemicals, insect droppings, diesel smoke and volcanic ash.

Using 'Like to Treat Like'

Unlike conventional medicines that suppress symptoms, homeopathic remedies treat illnesses with small doses of substances that, if administered in larger quantities, would produce the symptoms that the patient already has. Whilst the same homeopathic remedy can be used to treat different symptoms in different dogs, here are some interesting remedies and their uses.

Apis Mellifica
(made from honey bee venom) can be used for allergies or to reduce swelling that occurs in acutely infected kidneys.

Diesel Smoke
can be used to help control travel sickness.

Calcarea Fluorica
(made from calcium fluoride, which helps harden bone structure) can be useful in treating hard lumps in tissues.

Natrum Muriaticum
(made from common salt, sodium chloride) is useful in treating thin, thirsty dogs.

Nitricum Acidum
(made from nitric acid) is used for symptoms you would expect to see from contact with acids, such as lesions, especially where the skin joins the linings of body orifices or openings such as the lips and nostrils.

Symphytum
(made from the herb Knitbone, *Symphytum officianale*) is used to encourage bones to heal.

Urtica Urens
(made from the common stinging nettle) is used in treating painful, irritating rashes.

HOMEOPATHIC REMEDIES FOR YOUR DOG

Symptom/Ailment	Possible Remedy
ALLERGIES	Apis Mellifica 30c, Astacus Fluviatilis 6c, Pulsatilla 30c, Urtica Urens 6c
ALOPAECIA	Alumina 30c, Lycopodium 30c, Sepia 30c, Thallium 6c
ANAL GLANDS (BLOCKED)	Hepar Sulphuris Calcareum 30c, Sanicula 6c, Silicea 6c
ARTHRITIS	Rhus Toxicodendron 6c, Bryonia Alba 6c
CATARACT	Calcarea Carbonica 6c, Conium Maculatum 6c, Phosphorus 30c, Silicea 30c
CONSTIPATION	Alumina 6c, Carbo Vegetabilis 30c, Graphites 6c, Nitricum Acidum 30c, Silicea 6c
COUGHING	Aconitum Napellus 6c, Belladonna 30c, Hyoscyamus Niger 30c, Phosphorus 30c
DIARRHOEA	Arsenicum Album 30c, Aconitum Napellus 6c, Chamomilla 30c, Mercurius Corrosivus 30c
DRY EYE	Zincum Metallicum 30c
EAR PROBLEMS	Aconitum Napellus 30c, Belladonna 30c, Hepar Sulphuris 30c, Tellurium 30c, Psorinum 200c
EYE PROBLEMS	Borax 6c, Aconitum Napellus 30c, Graphites 6c, Staphysagria 6c, Thuja Occidentalis 30c
GLAUCOMA	Aconitum Napellus 30c, Apis Mellifica 6c, Phosphorus 30c
HEAT STROKE	Belladonna 30c, Gelsemium Sempervirens 30c, Sulphur 30c
HICCOUGHS	Cinchona Deficinalis 6c
HIP DYSPLASIA	Colocynthis 6c, Rhus Toxicodendron 6c, Bryonia Alba 6c
INCONTINENCE	Argentum Nitricum 6c, Causticum 30c, Conium Maculatum 30c, Pulsatilla 30c, Sepia 30c
INSECT BITES	Apis Mellifica 30c, Cantharis 30c, Hypericum Perforatum 6c, Urtica Urens 30c
ITCHING	Alumina 30c, Arsenicum Album 30c, Carbo Vegetabilis 30c, Hypericum Perforatum 6c, Mezerium 6c, Sulphur 30c
KENNEL COUGH	Drosera 6c, Ipecacuanha 30c
MASTITIS	Apis Mellifica 30c, Belladonna 30c, Urtica Urens 1m
PATELLAR LUXATION	Gelsemium Sempervirens 6c, Rhus Toxicodendron 6c
PENIS PROBLEMS	Aconitum Napellus 30c, Hepar Sulphuris Calcareum 30c, Pulsatilla 30c, Thuja Occidentalis 6c
PUPPY TEETHING	Calcarea Carbonica 6c, Chamomilla 6c, Phytolacca 6c
TRAVEL SICKNESS	Cocculus 6c, Petroleum 6c

Recognising a Sick Dog

Unlike colicky babies and cranky children, our canine kids cannot tell us when they are feeling ill. Therefore, there are a number of signs that owners can identify to know that their dogs are not feeling well.

Take note for physical manifestations such as:

- unusual, bad odour, including bad breath
- excessive moulting
- wax in the ears, chronic ear irritation
- oily, flaky, dull haircoat
- mucous, tearing or similar discharge in the eyes
- fleas or mites
- mucous in stool, diarrhoea
- sensitivity to petting or handling
- licking at paws, scratching face, etc.

Keep an eye out for behavioural changes as well including:

- lethargy, idleness
- lack of patience or general irritability
- lack of appetite, digestive problems
- phobias (fear of people, loud noises, etc.)
- strange behaviour, suspicion, fear
- coprophagia
- more frequent barking
- whimpering, crying

Get Well Soon

You don't need a DVR or a BVMA to provide good TLC to your sick or recovering dog, but you do need to pay attention to some details that normally wouldn't bother him. The following tips will aid Fido's recovery and get him back on his paws again:

- Keep his space free of irritating smells, like heavy perfumes and air fresheners.
- Rest is the best medicine! Avoid harsh lighting that will prevent your dog from sleeping. Shade him from bright sunlight during the day and dim the lights in the evening.
- Keep the noise level down. Animals are more sensitive to sound when they are sick.

- Be attentive to any necessary temperature adjustments. A dog with a fever needs a cool room and cold liquids. A bitch that is whelping or recovering from surgery will be more comfortable in a warm room, consuming warm liquids and food.
- You wouldn't send a sick child back to school early, so don't rush your dog back into a full routine until he seems absolutely ready.

Number-One Killer Disease in Dogs: CANCER

In every age there is a word associated with a disease or plague that causes humans to shudder. In the 21st century, that word is 'cancer.' Just as cancer is the leading cause of death in humans, it claims nearly half the lives of dogs that die from a natural disease as well as half the dogs that die over the age of ten years.

Described as a genetic disease, cancer becomes a greater risk as the dog ages. Veterinary surgeons and dog owners have become increasingly aware of the threat of cancer to dogs. Statistics reveal that one dog in every five will develop cancer, the most common of which is skin cancer. Many cancers, including prostate, ovarian and breast cancer, can be avoided by spaying and neutering our dogs by the age of six months.

Early detection of cancer can save or extend your dog's life, so it is absolutely vital for owners to have their dogs examined by a qualified veterinary surgeon or oncologist immediately upon detection of any abnormality. Certain dietary guidelines have also proven to reduce the onset and spread of cancer. Foods based on fish rather than beef, due to the presence of Omega-3 fatty acids, are recommended. Other amino acids such as glutamine have significant benefits for canines, particularly those breeds that show a greater susceptibility to cancer.

Cancer management and treatments promise hope for future generations of canines. Since the disease is genetic, breeders should never breed a dog whose parents, grandparents and any related siblings have developed cancer. It is difficult to know whether to exclude an otherwise healthy dog from a breeding programme, as the disease does not manifest itself until the dog's senior years.

RECOGNISE CANCER WARNING SIGNS

Since early detection can possibly rescue your dog from becoming a cancer statistic, it is essential for owners to recognise the possible signs and seek the assistance of a qualified professional.

- Abnormal bumps or lumps that continue to grow
- Bleeding or discharge from any body cavity
- Persistent stiffness or lameness
- Recurrent sores or sores that do not heal
- Inappetence
- Breathing difficulties
- Weight loss
- Bad breath or odours
- General malaise and fatigue
- Eating and swallowing problems
- Difficulty urinating and defecating

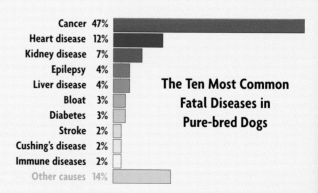

Disease	%
Cancer	47%
Heart disease	12%
Kidney disease	7%
Epilepsy	4%
Liver disease	4%
Bloat	3%
Diabetes	3%
Stroke	2%
Cushing's disease	2%
Immune diseases	2%
Other causes	14%

The Ten Most Common Fatal Diseases in Pure-bred Dogs

CDS: COGNITIVE DYSFUNCTION SYNDROME

'OLD-DOG SYNDROME'

There are many ways to evaluate old-dog syndrome. Veterinary surgeons have defined CDS (cognitive dysfunction syndrome) as the gradual deterioration of cognitive abilities. These are indicated by changes in the dog's behaviour. When a dog changes its routine response, and maladies have been eliminated as the cause of these behavioural changes, then CDS is the usual diagnosis.

More than half the dogs over eight years old suffer from some form of CDS. The older the dog, the more chance it has of suffering from CDS. In humans, doctors often dismiss the CDS behavioural changes as part of 'winding down.'

There are four major signs of CDS: the dog has frequent toilet accidents inside the home, sleeps much more or much less than normal, acts confused and fails to respond to social stimuli.

SYMPTOMS OF CDS

FREQUENT TOILET ACCIDENTS
- Urinates in the house.
- Defecates in the house.
- Doesn't signal that he wants to go out.

SLEEP PATTERNS
- Moves much more slowly.
- Sleeps more than normal during the day.
- Sleeps less during the night.

CONFUSION
- Goes outside and just stands there.
- Appears confused with a faraway look in his eyes.
- Hides more often.
- Doesn't recognise friends.
- Doesn't come when called.
- Walks around listlessly and without a destination.

FAILS TO RESPOND TO SOCIAL STIMULI
- Comes to people less frequently, whether called or not.
- Doesn't tolerate petting for more than a short time.
- Doesn't come to the door when you return home.

Your Veteran
BLOODHOUND

The term 'old' is a qualitative term. For dogs, as well as for their masters, old is relative. Certainly we can all distinguish between a puppy Bloodhound and an adult Bloodhound—there are the obvious physical traits, such as size, appearance and facial expressions, and personality traits. Puppies and young dogs like to play with children. Children's natural exuberance is a good match for the seemingly endless energy of young dogs. They like to run, jump, chase and retrieve. When dogs grow older and cease their interaction with children, they are often thought of as being too old to keep pace with young people. On the other hand, if a Bloodhound is only exposed to older people or quieter lifestyles, his life will normally be less active and the decrease in his activity level as he ages will not be as obvious.

If people live to be 100 years old, dogs live to be 20 years old. While this might seem like a good rule of thumb, it is very inaccurate. When trying to compare dog years to human years, you cannot make a generalisation about all dogs. Unfortunately, the

Bloodhound is not one of the longer-lived breeds of dog, though they can live to be ten years of age; as with many large breeds, six to eight years of age is much more common.

Dogs generally are considered physically mature at three years of age (or earlier), but can reproduce even earlier. So the first three years of a dog's life are like seven times that of comparable humans. That means a 3-year-old dog is like a 21-year-old human. As the curve of comparison shows, there is no hard and fast rule for comparing dog and human ages. Small breeds tend to live longer than large breeds, some breeds' adolescent periods last longer than others' and some breeds experience rapid periods of growth. The comparison is made even more difficult, for, likewise, not all humans age at the same rate...and human females live longer than human males.

WHAT TO LOOK FOR IN SENIORS

Most veterinary surgeons and breeders use the six-year mark as the time to consider a Bloodhound a 'senior' or 'veteran.'

Neither term implies that the dog is geriatric and has begun to fail in mind and body. Ageing is essentially a slowing process. Humans readily admit that they feel a difference in their activity level from age 20 to 30, and then from 30 to 40, etc. By treating the six-year-old dog as a senior, owners are able to implement certain therapeutic and preventative medical strategies with the help of their veterinary surgeons.

A senior-care programme should include at least two veterinary visits per year and screening sessions to determine the dog's health status, as well as nutritional counselling. Veterinary surgeons determine the senior dog's health status through a blood smear for a complete blood count, serum chemistry profile with electrolytes, urinalysis, blood pressure check, electrocardiogram, ocular tonometry (pressure on the eyeball) and dental prophylaxis.

Such an extensive programme for senior dogs is well advised before owners start to see the obvious physical signs of ageing, such as slower and inhibited movement, greying, increased sleep/nap periods and disinterest in play and other activity. This

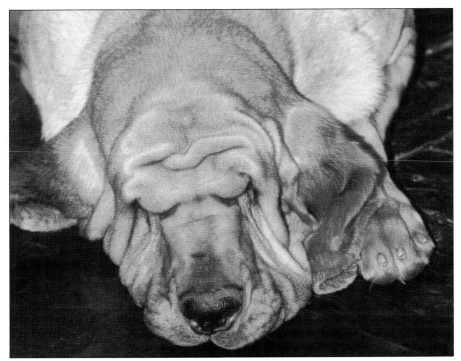

Senior Bloodhounds will sleep more frequently and for longer periods. No two dogs age at the exact same rate, so each Bloodhound will need to accessed by a vet to determine what modifications in his diet and care regimen are advisable.

preventative programme aims for a longer, healthier life for the ageing dog. Among the physical problems common in ageing dogs are the loss of sight and hearing, arthritis, kidney and liver failure, diabetes mellitus, heart disease and Cushing's disease (an hormonal disease).

In addition to the physical manifestations discussed, there are some behavioural changes and problems related to ageing dogs. Dogs suffering from hearing or vision loss, dental discomfort or arthritis can become aggressive. Likewise, the near-deaf and/or blind dog may be startled more easily and react in an unexpectedly aggressive manner. Seniors suffering from senility can become more impatient and irritable. Housesoiling accidents are associated with loss of mobility, kidney problems and loss of sphincter control as well as plaque accumulation, physiological brain changes and reactions to medications. Older dogs, just like young puppies, suffer from separation anxiety, which can lead to excessive barking, whining, housesoiling and destructive behaviour. Seniors may become fearful of everyday sounds, such as vacuum cleaners, heaters, thunder and passing traffic. Some dogs have difficulty sleeping, due to discomfort, the need for frequent toilet visits and the like. Owners should avoid spoiling

the older dog with too many fatty treats. Obesity is a common problem in older dogs and subtracts years from their lives. Keep the senior dog as trim as possible, since excessive weight puts additional stress on the body's vital organs. Some breeders recommend supplementing the diet with foods high in fibre and lower in calories. Adding fresh vegetables and marrow broth to the senior's diet makes a tasty, low-calorie, low-fat supplement. Vets also offer speciality diets for senior dogs that are worth exploring.

Your dog, as he nears his twilight years, needs your patience and good care more than ever. Never punish an older dog for an accident or abnormal behaviour. For the years of love, protection and companionship that your dog has provided, he deserves special attention and courtesies. The older dog may need to relieve himself at 3 a.m. because he can no longer hold it for eight hours. Older dogs may not be able to remain crated for more than two or three hours. It may be time to give up a sofa or chair to your old friend. Although he may not seem as enthusiastic about your attention and petting, he does appreciate the considerations you offer as he gets older.

Your Bloodhound does not understand why his world is slowing down. Owners must make their dogs' transition into their golden years as pleasant and rewarding as possible.

WHAT TO DO WHEN THE TIME COMES

You are never fully prepared to make a rational decision about putting your dog to sleep. It is very obvious that you love your Bloodhound or you would not be reading this book. Putting a beloved dog to sleep is extremely difficult. It is a decision that must be made with your veterinary surgeon. You are usually forced to make the decision when your dog experiences one or more life-threatening symptoms that have become serious enough for you to seek medical (veterinary) help.

If the prognosis of the malady indicates that the end is near and that your beloved pet will only continue to suffer and experience no enjoyment for the balance of its life, then euthanasia is the right choice.

WHAT IS EUTHANASIA?

Euthanasia derives from the Greek, meaning 'good death.' In other words, it means the planned, painless killing of a dog suffering from a painful, incurable condition, or who is so aged that it cannot walk, see, eat or control its excretory functions. Euthanasia is usually accomplished by injection with an overdose of anaesthesia or a barbiturate. Aside from the prick of the needle, the experience is usually painless.

MAKING THE DECISION

The decision to euthanise your dog is never easy. The days during which the dog becomes ill and the end occurs can be unusually stressful for you. If this is your first experience with the death of a loved one, you may need the comfort dictated by your religious beliefs. If you are the head of the family and have children, you should have involved them in the decision of putting your Bloodhound to sleep. Usually your dog can be maintained on drugs for a few days in order to give you ample time to make a decision. During this time, talking with members of your family or with people who have lived through the same experience can ease the burden of your inevitable decision.

THE FINAL RESTING PLACE

Dogs can have some of the same privileges as humans. The remains of your beloved dog can be buried in a pet cemetery, which is generally expensive. Dogs who have died at home can be buried in your garden in a place suitably marked with some stone or newly planted tree or bush. Alternatively, your dog can be cremated individually and the ashes returned to you. A less expensive option is mass

Many cities
have pet
cemeteries
conveniently
located. Your
veterinary
surgeon can
assist you in
locating one.

Many cities have pet cemeteries conveniently located. Your veterinary surgeon can assist you in locating one.

cremation, although, of course, the ashes cannot then be returned. Vets can usually arrange the cremation on your behalf. The cost of these options should always be discussed frankly and openly with your veterinary surgeon. In Britain, if your dog has died at the surgery, the vet legally cannot allow you to take your dog's body home.

GETTING ANOTHER DOG?
The grief of losing your beloved dog will be as lasting as the grief of losing an human friend or relative. In most cases, if your dog died of old age (if there is such a thing), it had slowed down considerably. Do you want a new Bloodhound puppy to replace it? Or are you better off finding a

more mature Bloodhound, say two to three years of age, which will usually be house-trained and will have an already developed personality. In this case, you can find out if you like each other after a few hours of being together.

The decision is, of course, your own. Do you want another Bloodhound or perhaps a different breed so as to avoid comparison with your beloved friend? Most people usually buy the same breed because they know (and love) the characteristics of that breed. Then, too, they often know people who have the same breed and perhaps they are lucky enough that one of their friends expects a litter soon. What could be better?

Showing Your
BLOODHOUND

If you purchased your Bloodhound with the hope of showing him in the conformation ring, you no doubt discussed your intentions with your breeder. Breeders who raise show-quality Bloodhounds can be an invaluable source of information and advice on how to prepare your puppy and adult dog for the show ring, as well as the protocol involved in this popular sporting event. You can also gain important insight and experience by exploring dog shows and visiting the rings where the Hound breeds are exhibited. Talk to the handlers and exhibitors and read all the literature that is often available at no charge at most show sites.

The first concept that the canine novice learns when watching a dog show is that each dog first competes against members of its own breed. Once the judge has selected the best member of each breed (Best of Breed), provided that the show is judged on a Group system, that chosen dog will compete with other dogs in its group. Finally, the best of each group will compete for Best in Show and Reserve Best in Show.

The second concept that you must understand is that the dogs are not actually compared against one another. The judge compares each dog against its breed standard, which is a written description of the ideal specimen of the breed. While some early breed standards were indeed based on specific dogs that were famous or popular, many dedicated enthusiasts say that a perfect specimen, as described in the standard, has never walked into a show ring, has never been bred and, to the woe of dog breeders around the globe, does not exist. Breeders attempt to get as close to this ideal as possible with every litter, but theoretically the 'perfect' dog is so elusive that it is impossible. (And if the 'perfect' dog were born, breeders and judges would never agree that it was indeed 'perfect.')

Serious show enthusiasts can also join a local or regional breed club. These clubs host Championship and Open Shows as well as Match meetings and other special events to provide practice forums for their members

SHOW QUALITY SHOWS

While you may purchase a puppy in the hope of having a successful career in the show ring, it is impossible to tell, at eight to ten weeks of age, whether your dog will be a contender. Some promising pups end up with minor to serious faults that prevent them from taking home a Best of Breed award, but this certainly does not mean they can't be the best of companions for you and your family. To find out if your potential show dog is show quality, enter him in a match to see how a judge evaluates him. You may also take him back to your breeder as he matures to see what he might advise.

different judges, with one win occurring after one year of age. CCs are awarded to the Best of Sex winners of each breed shown. Challenge Certificates are offered only at the three types of Championship Shows: the all-breed General Championship Shows for all Kennel-Club-recognised breeds; the Group Championship Shows, which are limited to certain breeds within a specific group; and the Breed Shows, which are open to a single breed.

The Kennel Club determines which breeds at which Championship Shows will have

and, more importantly, to help acquaint the novice with the intricacies of showing dogs.

Club events are governed by The Kennel Club, which is the ruling body for the British dog world. The Kennel Club dictates the rules and regulations not only for conformation shows but also for obedience shows, field trials and agility trials. Kennel Club authority also extends to dog shows in Australia, South Africa and many countries on other continents.

To become a Show Champion, a dog must earn three Challenge Certificates (CCs) under three

INFORMATION ON CLUBS

You can get information about dog shows from kennel clubs and breed clubs:

The Kennel Club
1-5 Clarges St., Piccadilly, London W1Y 8AB, UK
www.the-kennel-club.org.uk

Fédération Cynologique Internationale
14, rue Leopold II, B-6530 Thuin, Belgium
www.fci.be

American Kennel Club
5580 Centerview Dr., Raleigh, NC 27606-3390 USA
www.akc.org

Canadian Kennel Club
89 Skyway Ave., Suite 100, Etobicoke, Ontario
M9W 6R4 Canada
www.ckc.ca

Whether you are a novice exhibitor or a seasoned professional, the sport of dog showing offers much excitement and camaraderie.

the opportunity to earn Challenge Certificates (also called tickets). Serious exhibitors often will opt not to participate if the tickets are withheld at a particular show. This policy makes earning championships even more difficult to accomplish.

Open Shows are practice events that are less competitive and do not offer tickets. There are hundreds of Open Shows each year that can be delightful social events and are great first-show experiences for the novice. Even if you're considering just watching a show to wet your paws, an Open Show is a great choice.

While Championship and Open Shows are most important for the beginner to understand, there are other types of shows in which the interested dog owner can participate. Training clubs sponsor Matches that can be entered on the day of the show for a nominal fee. In these introductory-level exhibitions, two dogs'

CLASSES AT DOG SHOWS

There can be as many as 18 classes per sex for your breed. Check the show schedule carefully to make sure that you have entered your dog in the appropriate class. The classes offered can include Minor Puppy (ages 6 to 9 months), Puppy (ages 6 to 12 months), Junior (ages 6 to 18 months) and Beginners (handler or dog never won first place), as well as the following, each of which is defined in the schedule: Maiden; Novice; Tyro; Debutant; Undergraduate; Graduate; Postgraduate; Minor Limit; Mid Limit; Limit; Open; Veteran; Stud Dog; Brood Bitch; Progeny; Brace and Team.

names are pulled out of a hat and 'matched,' the winner of that match goes on to the next round and eventually only one dog is left undefeated.

Exemption Shows are much more light-hearted affairs with usually only four pedigree classes and several 'fun' classes, all of which can be entered on the day of the show. Exemption Shows are sometimes held in conjunction with small agricultural shows and the proceeds must be given to a charity. Limited Shows are also available in small number. Entry is restricted to members of the club that hosts the show, although you can usually join the club when making an entry.

Before you actually step into the ring, you would be well advised to sit back and observe the judge's ring procedure. If it is your first time in the ring, do not be over-anxious and run to the front of the line. It is much better to stand back and study how the exhibitor in front of you is performing. The judge asks each handler to 'stand' the dog, hopefully showing the dog off to his best advantage. The judge will observe the dog from a distance and from different angles, and approach the dog to check his teeth, overall structure, alertness and muscle tone, as well as consider how well the dog 'conforms' to the standard. Most importantly, the judge will have the exhibitor move the dog around the ring in some pattern that he or she should specify (another advantage to not going first, but always listen since some judges change their directions—and the judge is always right!). Finally, the judge will give the dog one last look before moving on to the next exhibitor.

If you are not in the top three at your first show, do not be discouraged. Be patient and consistent, and you may eventually find yourself in the winning line-up. Remember that the winners were once in your shoes and have devoted many hours and much money to earn the placement. If you find that your dog is losing every time and never getting a nod, it may be time to consider a different dog sport or to just enjoy your Bloodhound as a pet.

Virtually all countries with a recognised speciality breed club (sometimes called a 'parent' club) offer show conformation competition specifically for and among Bloodhounds. Under direction of the club, other special events for man-trailing, tracking, obedience and agility may be offered as well, whether for titling or just for fun.

FOLLOW YOUR NOSE

Although there are a number of organised competitions available to owners of pure-bred dogs, Bloodhounds are not ideally

HOW TO ENTER A DOG SHOW
1. Obtain an entry form and show schedule from the Show Secretary.
2. Select the classes that you want to enter and complete the entry form.
3. Transfer your dog into your name at The Kennel Club. (Be sure that this matter is handled before entering.)
4. Find out how far in advance show entries must be made. Oftentimes it's more than a couple of months.

suited for most of these. Working trials, agility trials, obedience shows, field trials, etc., are designed to test dogs' abilities, all requiring much specialised training and considerable

financial and time investments. Beyond man-trailing events, the Bloodhound's life revolves around his master and family and community-oriented service skills like search and rescue, PAT therapy dog work, detection work, etc.

In the US, Bloodhounds excel at tracking trials, based on the same principals as man-trailing, the dog's natural ability to follow human scent. These trials, endorsed by the American Kennel Club (AKC), give the dog the opportunity to add tracking suffixes to their names. The titles are each based on one of the three levels of tracking trials: Tracking Dog (TD), Tracking Dog Excellent (TDX), Variable Surface Tracking (VST) are awarded based on the dog's performance, demonstrating

that the dog can locate an article that has been dropped by a track layer minutes or hours previously. The more difficult trials cover greater distances of time and space, possibly dropping a leather glove miles away three or four days prior on a less direct course with various scenting obstacles. The VST is awarded to a dog that demonstrates its ability to follow a track in an urban and wilderness setting. There are tracking clubs that can be contacted for more information, and these can be reached through the AKC.

FÉDÉRATION CYNOLOGIQUE INTERNATIONALE

Established in 1911, the Fédération Cynologique Internationale (FCI) represents the 'world kennel club.' This international body brings uniformity to the breeding, judging and showing

A bitch who excels in the show ring may also be a candidate for a breeding programme. Owners with hopes of pursuing a show career with their new charges should seek out the puppies of Bloodhounds who have won titles in the show ring.

of pure-bred dogs. Although the FCI originally included only five European nations: France, Germany, Austria, the Netherlands and Belgium (which remains its headquarters), the organisation today embraces nations on six continents and recognises well over 300 breeds of pure-bred dog.

FCI sponsors both national and international shows. The hosting country determines the judging system and breed standards are always based on the breed's country of origin. Dogs from every country can participate in these impressive canine spectacles, the largest of which is the World Dog Show, hosted in a different country each year.

There are three titles attainable through the FCI: the International Champion, which is the most prestigious; the International Beauty Champion, which is based on aptitude certificates in different

> ### DID YOU KNOW?
> The FCI *does not* issue pedigrees. The FCI members and contract partners are responsible for issuing pedigrees and training judges in their own countries. The FCI does maintain a list of judges and makes sure that they are recognised throughout the FCI member countries.
>
> The FCI also *does not* act as a breeder referral; breeder information is available from FCI-recognised national canine societies in each of the FCI's member countries.

countries; and the International Trial Champion, which is based on achievement in obedience trials in different countries. The title of Champion at an FCI show requires a dog to win three CACs (*Certificats d'Aptitude au Championnat*), at regional or club shows under three different judges who are breed specialists. The title of International Champion is gained by winning four CACIBs (*Certificats d'Aptitude au Championnat International de Beauté*), which are offered only at international shows, with at least a one-year lapse between the first and fourth award.

The FCI is divided into ten Groups. At the World Dog Show, the following classes are offered for each breed: Puppy Class (6–9 months), Youth Class (9–18

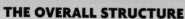

months), Open Class (15 months or older) and Champion Class. A dog can be awarded a classification of Excellent, Very Good, Good, Sufficient and Not Sufficient. Puppies can be awarded classifications of Very Promising, Promising or Not Promising. Four placements are made in each class. After all sexes and classes are judged, a Best of Breed is selected. Other special groups and classes may also be shown. Each exhibitor showing a dog receives a written evaluation from the judge.

Besides the World Dog Show and the European Championship Show and other all-breed shows, you can exhibit your dog at speciality shows held by different breed clubs. Speciality shows may have their own regulations.

FCI INFORMATION

There are 330 breeds recognised by the FCI, and each breed is considered to be 'owned' by a specific country. Each breed standard is a cooperative effort between the breed's country and the FCI's Standards and Scientific Commissions. Judges use these official breed standards at shows held in FCI member countries. One of the functions of the FCI is to update and translate the breed standards into French, English, Spanish and German.

THE OVERALL STRUCTURE

The overall structure of the FCI is divided into several bodies:
• General Assembly
• Executive Committee and General Committee
• Compulsory Commissions (Standards, Scientific and Legal)
• Non-compulsory Commissions

Awaiting her turn in the show ring, this Bloodhound sits in the benching area at a large all-breed show. Bench shows are ideal for visitors to meet the breeders and the dogs when they are not busy with the competition.

As a Bloodhound owner, you have selected your dog so that you and your loved ones can have a companion, a protector, a friend and a four-legged family member. You invest time, money and effort to care for and train the family's new charge. Of course, this chosen canine behaves perfectly! Well, perfectly like a *dog*.

THINK LIKE A DOG

Dogs do not think like humans, nor do humans think like dogs, though we try. Unfortunately, a dog is incapable of compre-hending how humans think, so the responsibility falls on the owner to adopt a proper canine mindset. Dogs cannot rationalise, and dogs exist in the present moment. Many dog owners make the mistake in training of thinking that they can reprimand their dog for something he did a while ago. Basically, you cannot even reprimand a dog for something he did 20 seconds ago! Either catch him in the act or forget it! It is a waste of your and your dog's time—in his mind, you are reprimanding him for whatever he is doing at that moment.

The following behavioural problems represent some which owners most commonly encounter. Every dog is unique and every situation is unique. No author could purport for you to solve your Bloodhound's problems simply by reading a script. Here we outline some basic 'dogspeak' so that owners' chances of solving behavioural problems are increased.

Discuss bad habits with your veterinary surgeon and he can recommend a behavioural specialist to consult in appropriate cases. Since behavioural abnormalities are the main reason owners abandon their pets, we hope that you will make a valiant effort to solve your Bloodhound's problems. Patience and understanding are virtues that must dwell in every pet-loving household.

SEPARATION ANXIETY

Recognised by behaviourists as the most common form of stress for dogs, separation anxiety can also lead to destructive behaviours in your dog. It's more than your Bloodhound's howling his displeasure at your leaving the house and his being left alone. This is a normal reaction, no different from the child who cries as his mother leaves him on the first day at school. Separation anxiety is more serious. In fact, if you are constantly with your dog, he will come to expect you with him all of the time, making it even more traumatic for him when you are not there.

Obviously, you enjoy spending time with your dog, and he thrives on your love and attention. However, it should not become a dependent relationship in which he is heartbroken without you. This broken heart can also bring on destructive behaviour as well as loss of appetite, depression and lack of interest in play and interaction. Canine behaviourists have been spending much time and energy to help owners better understand the significance of this stressful condition.

One thing you can do to minimise separation anxiety is to make your entrances and exits as low-key as possible. Do not give your dog a long drawn-out goodbye, and do not overly lavish him with hugs and kisses when you return. This is giving in to the attention that he craves, and it will only make him miss it more when you are away. Another thing you can try is to give your dog a treat when you leave; this not

DID YOU KNOW?
The number of dogs that suffer from separation anxiety is on the rise as more and more pet owners find themselves at work all day. New attention is being paid to this problem, which is especially hard to diagnose since it is only evident when the dog is alone. Research is currently being done to help educate dog owners about separation anxiety and how they can help minimise this problem in their dogs.

only will keep him occupied and keep his mind off the fact that you have just left but also will help him associate your leaving with a pleasant experience.

You may have to accustom your dog to being left alone at intervals. Of course, when your dog starts whimpering as you approach the door, your first instinct will be to run to him and comfort him, but do not do it! Eventually he will adjust to your absence. His anxiety stems from being placed in an unfamiliar situation; by familiarising him with being alone, he will learn that he will survive. That is not to say you should purposely leave your dog home alone, but the dog needs to know that, while he can depend on you for his care, you do not have to be by his side 24 hours a day. Some behaviourists recommend tiring the dog out before you leave home—take him for a good long walk or engage in a game of fetch in the garden.

When the dog is alone in the house, he should be placed in his crate—another distinct advantage to crate training your dog. The crate should be placed in his familiar happy family area, where he normally sleeps and already feels comfortable, thereby making him feel more at ease when he is alone. Be sure to give the dog a special chew toy to enjoy while he settles into his crate.

DID YOU KNOW?

There are two drugs specifically designed to treat mental problems in dogs. About 7 million dogs each year are destroyed because owners can no longer tolerate their dogs' behaviour, according to Nicholas Dodman, a specialist in animal behaviour at Tufts University in Massachusetts.

The first drug, Clomicalm, is prescribed for dogs suffering from 'separation anxiety,' which is said to cause them to react when left alone by barking, chewing their owners' belongings, drooling copiously or defecating or urinating inside the home.

The second drug, Anipryl, is recommended for canine cognitive dysfunction or 'old dog syndrome,' a mental deterioration that comes with age. Such dogs often seem to forget that they were house-trained and where their food bowls are, and they may even fail to recognise their owners.

A tremendous human-animal bonding relationship is established with all dogs, particularly senior dogs. This precious relationship deteriorates when the dog does not recognise his master. The drug can restore the bond and make senior dogs feel more like their old selves.

Some Bloodhounds will go to great lengths to communicate with their human masters.

I'M HOME!

Dogs left alone for varying lengths of time may often react wildly when their owners return. Sometimes they run, jump, bite, chew, tear things apart, wet themselves, gobble their food or behave in very undisciplined ways. If your dog behaves in this manner upon your return home, allow him to calm down before greeting him or he will consider your attention as a reward for his antics.

BARKING

Blest with a booming hound voice, the Bloodhound has a knack for expressing himself vocally. Barking is a dog's way of 'talking.' It can be somewhat frustrating because it is not always easy to tell what a dog means by his bark—is he excited, happy, frightened or angry? Whatever it is that the dog is trying to say, he should not be punished for barking. It is only when the barking becomes excessive, and when the excessive barking becomes a bad habit, that the behaviour needs to be modified.

Bloodhounds tend to be vocal when outdoors, especially when they are on a trail or have located their quarry. They have a resonant, melodious voice, a cross between baying and a sing-song howl.

Nevertheless, Bloodhounds use their sonorous voices for a purpose, more so than other scenthounds that tend to be more 'bark-happy.' If an intruder came into your home in the middle of the night and your Bloodhound barked a warning, wouldn't you be pleased? You would deem your dog a hero, a wonderful guardian and protector of the home. On the other hand, if a friend drops by

BARKING STANCE

Did you know that a dog is less likely to bark when sitting than standing? Watch your dog the next time that you suspect he is about to start barking. You'll notice that as he does, he gets up on all four feet. Hence, when teaching a dog to stop barking, it helps to get him to sit before you command him to be quiet.

DOG TALK

Deciphering your dog's barks is very similar to understanding a baby's cries: there is a different cry for eating, sleeping, toilet needs, etc. Your dog talks to you not only through howls and groans but also through his body language. Baring teeth, staring and inflating the chest are all threatening gestures. If a dog greets you by licking his nose, turning his head or yawning, these are friendly, peacemaking gestures.

distinguish your dog's different barks and their meanings. For example, the bark when someone comes to the door will be different from the bark when he is excited to see you. It is similar to a person's tone of voice, except that the dog has to rely totally on tone of voice because he does not have the benefit of using words. An incessant barker will be evident at an early age.

There are some things that encourage a dog to bark. For

unexpectedly, rings the doorbell and is greeted with a sudden bark, you would probably be annoyed at the dog. But in reality, isn't this just the same behaviour? The dog does not know any better. Unless he sees who is at the door and it is someone he knows, he will bark as a means of vocalising that his (and your) territory is being threatened. While your friend is not posing a threat, it is all the same to the dog. Barking is his means of letting you know that there is an intrusion, whether friend or foe, on your property. This type of barking is instinctive and should not be discouraged.

Excessive habitual barking, however, is a problem that should be corrected early on. As your Bloodhound grows up, you will be able to tell when his barking is purposeful and when it is for no reason. You will become able to

HE'S PROTECTING YOU

Barking is your dog's way of protecting you. If he barks at a stranger walking past your house, a moving car or a fleeing cat, he is merely exercising his responsibility to protect his pack (YOU) and territory from a perceived intruder. Since the 'intruder' usually keeps going, the dog thinks his barking chased it away and he feels fulfilled. This behaviour leads your overly vocal friend to believe that he is the 'dog in charge.'

PROFESSIONAL TRAINING

If your dog barks menacingly or growls at strangers, or if he growls at anyone who comes near him while he is eating, playing with a toy or taking a rest in his favourite spot, he needs proper professional training because sooner or later this behaviour can result in someone's being bitten.

example, if your dog barks non-stop for a few minutes and you give him a treat to quieten him, he believes that you are rewarding him for barking. He will associate barking with getting a treat and will keep doing it until he is rewarded. On the other hand, if you give him a command such as 'Quiet' and praise him after he has stopped barking for a few seconds, he will get the idea that being 'quiet' is what you want him to do.

AGGRESSION

Although the temperament of the Bloodhound has improved greatly in modern times, aggression is a problem that concerns all responsible dog owners, especially owners of large, powerful dogs. Aggression can be a very big problem in dogs, and, when not controlled, always becomes dangerous. An aggressive dog, no matter the size, may lunge at, bite or even attack a person or another

dog. Aggressive behaviour is not to be tolerated. It is more than just inappropriate behaviour; it is painful for a family to watch their dog become unpredictable in his behaviour to the point where they are afraid of him. While not all aggressive behaviour is dangerous, growling, baring teeth, etc., can be frightening. It is important to ascertain why the dog is acting in this manner. Aggression is a display of dominance, and the dog should not have the dominant role in its pack, which is, in this case, your family.

It is important not to challenge an aggressive dog, as this could provoke an attack. Observe your Bloodhound's body language. Does he make direct eye contact and stare? Does he try to make himself as large as possible: head high, chest out, tail erect? Height and size signify authority in a dog pack—being taller or 'above' another dog literally means that he is 'above' in social status. These body signals tell you that your Bloodhound thinks he is in charge, a problem that needs to be addressed. An aggressive dog is unpredictable; you never know when he is going to strike and what he is going to do. You cannot understand why a dog that is playful one minute is growling the next.

Fear is a common cause of

aggression in dogs. Perhaps your Bloodhound had a negative experience as a puppy, which causes him to be fearful when a similar situation presents itself later in life. The dog may act aggressively in order to protect himself from whatever is making him afraid. It is not always easy to determine what is making your dog fearful, but if you can isolate what brings out the fear reaction, you can help the dog get over it.

Supervise your Bloodhound's interactions with people and other dogs, and praise the dog when it goes well. If he starts to act aggressively in a situation, correct him and remove him from the situation. Do not let people approach the dog and start petting him without your express permission. That way, you can have the dog sit to accept petting, and praise him when he behaves properly. You are focusing on praise and on modifying his behaviour by rewarding him when he acts appropriately. By being gentle and by supervising his interactions, you are showing him that there is no need to be afraid or defensive.

The best solution is to consult a behavioural specialist, one who has experience with the Bloodhound if possible. Together, perhaps you can pinpoint the cause of your dog's aggression and do something about it. An aggressive dog cannot be trusted,

and a dog that cannot be trusted is not safe to have as a family pet. If, very unusually, you find that your pet has become untrustworthy and you feel it necessary to seek a new home with a more suitable family and environment, explain fully to the new owners all your reasons for rehoming the dog to be fair to all concerned. In the very worst case, you will have to consider euthanasia.

AGGRESSION TOWARD OTHER DOGS
A dog's aggressive behaviour toward another dog stems from not enough exposure to other dogs at an early age. If other dogs make your Bloodhound nervous and agitated, he will lash out as a protective mechanism. A dog that has not received sufficient exposure to other canines tends to think that he is the only dog on the planet. The animal becomes so dominant that he does not even show signs that he is fearful or threatened. Without growling or any other physical signal as a warning, he will lunge at and bite the other dog.

A way to correct this is to let your Bloodhound approach another dog when walking on lead. Watch very closely and, at the first sign of aggression, correct your Bloodhound and pull him away. Scold him for any sign of discomfort, and then praise him when he ignores the other dog. Keep this up until either he stops the aggressive behaviour, learns to ignore other dogs or even accepts other dogs. Praise him lavishly for his correct behaviour.

SEXUAL BEHAVIOUR

Dogs exhibit certain sexual behaviours that may have influenced your choice of male or female when you first purchased your Bloodhound. To a certain extent, spaying/neutering will eliminate these behaviours, but if you are purchasing a dog that you wish to breed from, you should be aware of what you will have to deal with throughout the dog's life.

Female dogs usually have two oestruses per year, with each season lasting about three weeks. These are the only times in which a female dog will mate, and she usually will not allow this until the second week of the cycle, although this varies from bitch to bitch. If not bred during the heat cycle, it is not uncommon for a bitch to experience a false pregnancy, in which her mammary glands swell and she exhibits maternal tendencies toward toys or other objects.

With male dogs, owners must aware that whole dogs (dogs who are not neutered) have the natural inclination to mark their territory. Males mark their territory by spraying small amounts of urine as they lift their legs in a macho

ritual. Marking can occur both outdoors in the garden and around the neighbourhood as well as indoors on furniture legs, curtains and the sofa. Such behaviour can be very frustrating for the owner; early training is strongly urged before the 'urge' strikes your dog. Neutering the male at an appropriate early age can solve this problem before it becomes a habit.

Other problems associated with males are wandering and mounting. Both of these habits, of course, belong to the unneutered dog, whose sexual drive leads him away from home in search of the bitch in heat. Males will mount females in heat, as well as any other dog, male or female, that happens to catch their fancy. Other possible mounting partners include his owner, the furniture, guests to the home and strangers on the street. Discourage such behaviour early on.

Owners must further recognise that mounting is not merely a sexual expression but also one of dominance seen in dogs and bitches alike. Be consistent and be persistent, and you will find that you can 'move mounters.'

CHEWING

The national canine pastime is chewing! Every dog loves to sink his 'canines' into a tasty bone, but sometimes that bone is in his owner's hand! Dogs need to chew, to massage their gums, to make their new teeth feel better and to exercise their jaws. This is a natural behaviour that is deeply embedded in all things canine. Our role as owners is not to stop the dog's chewing, but rather to redirect it to positive, chew-worthy objects. Be an informed owner and purchase proper chew toys, like strong nylon bones, that will not splinter. Be sure that the objects are safe and durable, since your dog's safety is at risk. Again, the owner is responsible for ensuring a dog-proof environment.

The best answer is prevention; that is, put your shoes, handbags and other tasty objects in their proper places (out of the reach of the growing canine mouth). Direct puppies to their toys whenever you see them 'tasting' the furniture legs or the leg of your trousers. Make a loud noise to attract the pup's attention and immediately escort him to his chew toy and engage him with the toy for at least four minutes, praising and encouraging him all the while. An array of safe, interesting chew toys will keep your dog's mind and teeth occupied and distracted from chewing on things he shouldn't.

Some trainers recommend deterrents, such as hot pepper, a bitter spice or a product designed for this purpose, to discourage the dog from chewing unwanted objects. Test these products to see which works best before investing in large quantities.

JUMPING UP

Jumping up is a dog's friendly way of saying hello—and when a Bloodhound stands on his hind legs, you listen! Some dog owners do not mind when their dog jumps up...although with a 45-kg dog, this is less than a brilliant idea.

Pick a command such as 'Off.' (avoid using 'Down' since you will use that for the dog to lie down) and tell him 'Off' when he jumps up. Place him on the ground on all fours and have him sit, praising him the whole time. Always lavish him with praise and petting when he is in the sit position. In this way, you can give him a warm, affectionate greeting, let him know that you are as excited to see him as he is to see you and instil good manners at the same time!

DIGGING

Digging, which is seen as a destructive behaviour to humans, is actually quite a natural behaviour in dogs. Although terriers (the 'earth dogs') are most associated with the digging, any dog's desire to dig can be irrepressible and most frustrating to his owners. When digging occurs in your garden, it is actually a normal behaviour redirected into something the dog can do in his everyday life. In the wild, a dog would be actively seeking food, making his own shelter, etc. He would be using his paws in a purposeful manner for his survival. Since you provide him with food and shelter, he has no need to use his paws for these purposes, and so the energy that he would be using may manifest itself in the form of little holes all over your garden and flower beds.

Perhaps your dog is digging as a reaction to boredom—it is somewhat similar to someone eating a whole bag of crisps in front of the TV—because they are there and there is nothing better to do! Basically, the answer is to provide the dog with adequate play and exercise so that his mind and paws are occupied, and so that he feels as if he is doing something useful.

Of course, digging is easiest to control if it is stopped as soon as possible, but it is often hard to catch a dog in the act. If your dog is a compulsive digger and is not easily distracted by other activities, you can designate an area on your property where he is allowed to dig. If you catch him digging in an off-limits area of the garden, immediately bring him to the approved area and praise him for digging there. Keep a close eye on him so that you can catch him in the act—that is the only way to make him understand what is permitted and what is not. If you take him to a hole he dug an hour ago and tell him 'No,' he will understand that you are not fond of holes, or dirt or flowers. If you catch him while he is stifle-deep in your tulips, that is when he will get your message.

FOOD STEALING

Is your dog devising ways of stealing food from your coffee table or kitchen counter? If so, you must answer the following questions: Is your Bloodhound hungry, or is he 'constantly famished' like many dogs seem to be? Face it, some dogs are more food-motivated than others. They are totally obsessed by the smell of food and can only think of their next meal. Food stealing is terrific fun and always yields a great reward— FOOD, glorious food!

Your goal as an owner, therefore, is to be sensible about where food is placed in the home and to reprimand your dog whenever he is caught in the act of stealing. But remember, only reprimand your dog if you actually see him stealing, not later when the crime is discovered; that will be of no use at all and will only serve to confuse him.

BEGGING

Just like food stealing, begging is a favourite pastime of hungry puppies! It achieves that same lovely result—FOOD! Dogs quickly learn that their owners keep the 'good food' for themselves, and that we humans do not dine on dried food alone. Begging is a conditioned response related to a specific stimulus, time and place. The sounds of the kitchen, cans and bottles opening, crinkling bags, the smell of food in preparation, etc., will excite the dog, and soon that awesome nose will be in the air!

Here is the solution to stopping this behaviour: Never give in to a beggar! You are rewarding the dog for sitting pretty, whining and rubbing his nose into you by giving him food. By ignoring the dog, you will (eventually) force the behaviour into extinction. Note that the behaviour is likely to get worse before it disappears, so be sure there are not any 'softies' in the family who will give in to 'Oliver' every time he whimpers, 'More, please.'

COPROPHAGIA

Faeces eating is, to humans, one of the most disgusting behaviours that their dogs could engage in, yet, to dogs, it is perfectly normal. It is hard for us to understand why a dog would want to eat his own faeces. He could be seeking certain nutrients that are missing from his diet, he could be just plain hungry or he could be attracted by the pleasing (to a dog) scent. While coprophagia most often refers to the dog's eating his own faeces, a dog may just as likely eat that of another animal as well if he comes across it.

Vets have found that diets with low levels of digestibility, containing relatively low levels of fibre and high levels of starch, increase coprophagia. Therefore, high-fibre diets may decrease the likelihood of dogs' eating faeces. Both the consistency of the stool (how firm it feels in the dog's mouth) and the presence of undigested nutrients increase the likelihood. Dogs often find the stool of cats and horses more palatable than that of other dogs. Once the dog develops diarrhoea from faeces eating, he will likely stop this distasteful habit.

To discourage this behaviour, first make sure that the food you are feeding your dog is nutritionally complete and that he is getting enough food. If changes in his diet do not seem to work, and no medical cause can be found, you will have to modify the behaviour through environmental control before it becomes a habit. The best way to prevent your dog from eating his stool is to make it unavailable—clean up after he eliminates and remove any stool from the garden. If it is not there, he cannot eat it. Reprimanding for stool eating rarely impresses the dog.

INDEX

Page numbers in **boldface** indicate illustrations.

My Bloodhound

PUT YOUR PUPPY'S FIRST PICTURE HERE

Dog's Name _____

Date _____ Photographer _____